HITS

I0809280

PETER SZENDY

HITS

PHILOSOPHY IN THE JUKEBOX

Translated by Will Bishop

FORDHAM UNIVERSITY PRESS)) NEW YORK)) 2012

Copyright © 2012 Fordham University Press

All rights reserved. No part of this publication may be reproduced, stored in a retrieval system, or transmitted in any form or by any means—electronic, mechanical, photocopy, recording, or any other—except for brief quotations in printed reviews, without the prior permission of the publisher.

This work was originally published in French as Peter Szendy, *Tubes: La Philosophie dans le juke-box* © 2008 Les Editions de Minuit. The final five essays have been added by the author for the English-language edition.

Ouvrage publié avec le concours du Ministère français chargé de la Culture–Centre National du Livre.

This work has been published with the assistance of the French Ministry of Culture–National Center for the Book.

Fordham University Press has no responsibility for the persistence or accuracy of URLs for external or third-party Internet websites referred to in this publication and does not guarantee that any content on such websites is, or will remain, accurate or appropriate.

Fordham University Press also publishes its books in a variety of electronic formats. Some content that appears in print may not be available in electronic books.

Library of Congress Cataloging-in-Publication Data is available from the publisher.

Printed in the United States of America

14 13 12 5 4 3 2 1

First edition

CONTENTS

PREFACE *Especially for the English-language Reader*

I would like to be able to tell you, dear reader, to declare to you: This book is for you.

All for you, especially for you, for you alone.

Yet by saying that it's *All for you*, whom might I already be citing? Janet Jackson, perhaps, who gave these words as a title to her 2001 album before it went on to sell over three million copies? By swearing that everything that follows was thought through *Especially for you*, what cover song am I already interpreting? Without knowing it, before even remembering it, am I not borrowing these words in advance from Kylie Minogue and her duet with Jason Donovan, which was a huge hit in 1998?

You and I, dear reader, are certainly not the first to notice the way the hit song especially addresses you and me, the way it addresses each one of us through what seems most singular about us. *Especially for you* was, for example, the title of one of the musical commodities (*musikalische Waren*) whose apostrophe was analyzed by Adorno in *Quasi una fantasia* with distrust and irony in order to denounce the illusion they produce.

> Anyone who had harboured the illusion that an object existed especially for him, and who had bought it on that

> assumption, will dismiss the idea that it actually belonged to him. He belongs to the product and not the product to him.[1]

What, then, dear reader, are you going to make of me if, in spite of it all, and whatever Adorno may say, I dare to address you as if there were *only you*?

You may suspect me of wanting to play surreptitiously on your—perhaps unconscious—familiarity with the unavoidable 1955 Platters song as a way of creating an artificial complicity between us. At which point, out of annoyance, you might want to reply by reversing Baudelaire's interpellation of his reader at the beginning of *The Flowers of Evil*: "Hypocritical reader," Baudelaire wrote, turning toward you; "hypocritical author," you could in turn say to me, attributing me with the intention of smuggling these pages into you by using the words of hits as subliminal advertisements.

I confess it to you directly, since, for a few paragraphs now, we have already struck up a certain intimacy: I have sometimes dreamed of a book that, a little bit like Alain Resnais's film *Same Old Song*, would be composed solely of the titles of hit songs: a vast cut-up and a gigantic collage of musical commodities that would all murmur, like Prince did on what would be his first album in 1978, *For You, I'm Yours. . . .* Imagine: Not only would each one of these singing ads claim to say, once again like Prince: *All of this and more is for you*; not only would each one of them whisper a voluptuous *Take me, baby, yeah, I'm yours* into your ear, but it would also just as immediately inspire in you the irrepressible mnemonic effect of which it is capable: A memory proper to you would be attached to each one, an unforgettable yet buried moment that would all of a sudden rise to the surface of your conscious memory. And each one would then become what the narrator of Poe's "The Imp of the Perverse" describes as "a haunting and harassing thought":

> It harassed because it haunted. I could scarcely get rid of it for an instant. It is quite a common thing to be thus annoyed with the ringing in our ears, or rather in our memories, of the burthen of some ordinary song, or some unimpressive snatches from an opera. Nor will we be less tormented if the song in itself be good, or the opera air meritorious.[2]

You will have by now understood, dear reader, that this kind of torture—voluptuous and cruel, but also very ordinary—is what the book in your hands is going to speak of. Even if, in the end, each one of its sentences is not borrowed from an identifiable hit, many passages will no doubt give rise within you to hauntings analogous to the ones evoked by Poe.

These melodic obsessions, these melobsessions living in the melomaniacs that we are—it is not a matter of protecting ourselves from them or defending ourselves against them, of trying to get rid of them or find a cure for them. It is also not a question of simply condemning the hypocrisy of hits' advertising address to their listener, all of their *Only you*'s and *Especially for you*'s, as Adorno thought he had to do in a gesture bathed in Enlightenment.

Quite to the contrary, the experiment I am proposing to you, to you and you alone, demands that you allow yourself to be taken away into the infinite wanderings and loops of melobsessive haunting as a way of experiencing it as the very structure of the psyche. Better yet: You will gain access to yourself in what you and I might call an *inthymnacy*, in other words an intimacy already expropriated by the market of musical exchanges that make it possible.

What awaits you is therefore not an Adornian unveiling of the hit's hypocrisy whenever it calls out to you, you and only you. It is rather the observation that the apostrophe is already ventriloquized by the musical commodity *when you address you yourself at your very most intimate*: When, to yourself, you say and whisper to yourself *Only you, especially for you . . .*

This book, as you now know, is thus all for you.

Of course, I must acknowledge that you will have to lend an ear to hits that a French or Italian audience probably knows better than you do. Here and there, you will have to work your way through songs that you perhaps don't know well enough for them truly to form the soundtrack to your life, for them to have, by virtue of simply being mentioned, the powerful and obsessive mnemonic effect they have on others than you: "Un air comme ça" by Boris Vian, "Mélodie interdite" by Serge Gainsbourg, "La donna cannone" by Francesco De Gregori . . .

Thinking especially of you, I could have tried to replace these pieces from the Italian or French songsters' repertoire with others that could have played the same exemplary role, while allowing me to count on a real familiarity with you. I don't know if you know, for example, "Parole, parole, parole," the masterpiece sung by Mina in 1971, which I auscultate to read in it what I call the self-desiring structure of the hit. I could have spoken to you instead of Mark Lawrence's "romantic comedy," *Music and Lyrics* (2007). The song—the hit for which the film is a kind of "making of"—is also divided into words and music, with its two protagonists being respectively incarnated on the screen as melody and words personified: Alex (Hugh Grant) is a washed-up singer, while Sophie (Drew Barrymore) is his makeshift lyricist. The two of them act out the same scene we find in "Parole, parole, parole": a desiring game, a chase scene made up of the attractions and escapes between *melos* and *logos.*

But it was not a question of writing another book based on another hit parade. I therefore chose, without changing anything in what was written, to add for you several essays and chapters that were not included in the French version of the book. Besides Hitchcock, Pink Floyd, John Lennon, Ray Charles, and all the others you will have encountered, you will also find *in fine* two characters that you probably already know: Kafka's *Josephine*, whose vocal banality I understand in an entirely different way from the way Žižek understands it,[3] and the king of pop, Michael Jackson, whom you will rediscover transformed and transfigured into capital's Thing.

See, I told you: It's especially for you.

CHAPTER 1 Earworms: Life's Soundtrack

Like me, I am sure, you have all been haunted, obsessed to the point of queasiness, possessed until you just can't take it any more by one of those tunes that come to you *just like that*, one of those songs you hear by chance (which means, of course, by necessity) on the radio, in a café, or at the supermarket: one of those *hits* that, from that moment on, refuses to let you go. It is there on your lips when you wake up, it gives a beat to your steps in the street or else it comes to mind all of a sudden without your knowing why, interrupting your train of thought and the dreams of your innermost self.

You love them or hate them: You can hear them again years later and be engulfed by a wave of nostalgia that takes you back to a past moment as if you had never left it. You can also, on the contrary, devote all your forces to the attempt to defend yourself against this musical parasite that has dared take a hold of you. . . . Nothing is to be done: A kind of virus has taken over you and you have caught what some have called an *earworm*.

It was only recently that I came across this expression while reading the French translation of an article that appeared in the English daily, the *Guardian*.

> According to James Kellaris, marketing professor at the University of Cincinnati, . . . at one time or another nearly 99 percent of people have had earworms—those sticky tunes that people can't get out of their heads. . . . On average, the episodes may last several hours and happen quite frequently in "chronic sufferers." The term "earworm" is a translation of the German word *Ohrwurm,* used to describe the "musical itch" of the brain. . . . The musical earworm actually works more like a virus, attaching itself to a host and keeping itself alive by feeding off the host's memory.[1]

Even if the thought of consulting the "virtual clinic" this eminent academic has opened online would probably never have crossed my mind,[2] I do often suffer from earworms. Not so much the ones that are apparently at the top of the charts of our globalized obsessions (the *Guardian* cites Kylie Minogue's "Can't Get You Out of My Head," whose title, not without irony, is itself emblematic of the phenomenon), but others, whether ones I hold dear ("Parole, parole, parole," a veritable masterpiece) or ones that exasperate me ("Imagine," the intolerable "Imagine" by John Lennon). Have I then decided to write this book about and for them as a way of purging myself of them?

Perhaps.

But I have also written this book to give some dignity to these objects that are so often and in so many discourses considered as entirely lacking in merit. I even want to lend them a philosophical dignity, in something of the same way that ragpickers, kitsch, signs, ads, the mania for collecting, and children's books were elevated to the status of philosophical objects in the work of Walter Benjamin, both in *The Arcades Project* and elsewhere in his writing.

This is therefore an attempt to *think* hits. To trace a concept, a *logic* of the hit. And to give full entitlement to the *philosophical* surprise that accompanies the confrontation with something that seems so obvious: in other words, banality and singularity.

What does the triviality of the hit really hide when it can nonetheless move us as no one else can? What singular emotions are in play? What investments, what economies—both mercantile and psychic—are at work in them, and perhaps even what politics? In short, how is a *tune just like that*, a simple little tune that seems to come from nowhere and from everywhere at the same time, able to accompany our lives and constitute its incomparable soundtrack?[3] What makes it seem to harmonize with what is so proper to each one of us? How does it become the carrier or the repository of our incomparable passions, all while being inscribed in the circulation of a general exchange of clichés?

CHAPTER 2 *The Banal and the Singular*

A Tune Just Like That: The Secret of the Commodity

In 1958, a year before his death, Boris Vian wrote the following lyrics for a song Henri Salvador would later record (in 1979):

> Out onto the sidewalk she sends/A tune just like that/doo da da doo dah/Doo da da doodaia . . . —He came along whistling/A tune just like that/(*whistles* . . .)—They looked at each other with surprise./ She asked:/"How is it that you know it, I'm all agog . . ."/He answered:/(*spoken*) "Well, ah, I, ah, I actually don't know it,"/(*sung*) "It came just like that . . ."/Doo da da doo dah/Doo da doo da doo dah, doo da, doo da . . . .[1]

The tune is simple—it is indeed a tune *just like that.* A tune you sing while strolling down the street, a tune that comes to you *just like that,* without thinking about it, without wanting to, sometimes without even knowing or recognizing what it is. A tune that thus potentially has all the qualities—or all the absence of qualities—that might turn it into a *hit.*

This word—in French, *un tube*—was actually given its slang use in this sense by Boris Vian, who used it to refer to a success in the music industry.[2] He uses the word twice in *En avant la zizique . . .* , his "short treatise" on song.[3] He had also already used it as the title of another song he wrote for Henri Salvador in 1957, which lists the necessary ingredients, or rather the sufficient ingredients, for success.

So "The Hit," or in French "Le Tube," starts like this:

> "Here's what you need to have a hit./A street, a sidewalk, a nicely built girl./A guy with a black sweater and slicked-back hair./An old lingering refrain, neither sad nor gay . . . —That's all you need, Ladies and Gentlemen, come on in!/The girl and the guy, well, they just met./Between them, all of a sudden, something has clicked,/And now into the night they go . . ."[4]

The hit—the refrain that lingers without qualities and whose supreme characteristic seems to be not to have too many characteristics ("neither sad nor gay")—the hit would then be, says the song "The Hit" itself, the typical, general, and perhaps universal story of the event of an encounter. A banal love story, about which so many successful songs do indeed sing, often noting, as a matter of fact, their own banality. From Dalida's "L'Histoire d'un amour" (1958)[5] to Eddy Mitchell's "Je chante pour ceux qui ont le blues" (2003),[6] from B. B. King ("Same Old Story, Same Old Song") to Laurent Voulzy ("Désir désir"),[7] and countless others.

In the midst of this hit parade of songs willfully singing the banality of song (saying, each in its own way, that a song is always *the* song in general), "A Tune Just Like That," goes one step further, just like that. Like that, without seeming to, with a distance that resembles that taken by the flâneur, "A Tune Just Like That" stages an encounter that is not only the one between the girl and the guy, those necessary ingredients of a hit: Before the banal protagonists have even noticed it, the encounter in question, the encounter being depicted is the one between the song itself and its double or reincarnation, another version or metamorphosis of itself. The girl sings and the guy whistles at her; and, before they've even realized it, *just like that*, the tune has recognized itself. She is "struck dumb"; he is too, as he mumbles, "Well, ah, I, well, I don't know it, it came just like that . . ." They look at each other, "very surprised" by what seems obvious: Rather than providing the stage for their encounter, the song has already gone off on its own to meet itself, getting to know and recognizing itself.

Who is the flâneur in this case if not the tune itself? The tune is the one who seems to walk around, living its life, its autonomous life as a musical commodity, endowed with a soul and with movement. Perhaps, and we'll get to this later, with a *motive*, in the criminological sense of the word.

By speaking of itself, as do so many hits, this singular song, "The Hit" by Boris Vian, also speaks to us about musical commodities in general: about how they are made, manufactured, and produced. "Un air comme ça" ("A Tune Just Like That") takes this a step further by singing to us in its own way what Marx, in a famous passage of *Capital*, called the "secret" of the commodity.[8]

What exactly is this?

"A commodity," writes Marx, "appears, at first sight, a very trivial thing, and easily understood." It's something used to satisfy certain needs and, as such, seems to have nothing "mysterious" about it. Yet among the things that bear this "use value," the commodity, as such, behaves in a remarkable way. As Marx himself nicely says with his example of an ordinary table, as a commodity, the table "evolves out of its wooden brain grotesque ideas, far more wonderful than 'table-turning' ever was." For the table-commodity, like all commodities, is not only a useful thing: It also includes, summarizes, or incarnates a "definite social relation between men" (*das bestimmte gesellschaftliche Verhältnis der Menschen selbst*, 19), in other words a certain type of relationship between those who produce it with their labor. A commodity, for example, is the product or the expression of a certain amount of labor and of a certain way of organizing that labor. Yet this social relationship, which is in a way retained by the commodity, is also forgotten in it: For humans, it takes on "the fantastic form of a relation between things" (*die phantasmagorische Form eines Verhältnisses von Dingen*, 19). And it is the capacity of products to appear as "independent beings" that Marx calls "the Fetishism [*Fetischismus*] which attaches itself to the products of labor."

> To [producers], therefore, the relations connecting the labor of one individual with that of the rest appear, not as direct social relations between individuals at work, but as what they really are . . . , social relations between things. (19)

It is indeed the case that on the exchange market, a commodity lives thanks to its exchange value, one that seems *uniquely its own*, a kind of property it naturally has while it remains oblivious to the relations of production that gave it its existence. The commodity seems to have its own autonomous movement and reasoning when it circulates from exchange to exchange. Like a fake fetish, the commodity therefore seems to have a psyche, that "soul of the commodity" (*Warenseele*) ironically invoked by Marx. As a way of better showing up this illusion, Marx makes this soul speak.

> Could commodities themselves speak, they would say: Our use-value [*Gebrauchswert*] may be a thing that interests men. It is no part of us as objects. What, however, does belong to us as objects, is our value [*Wert*]. Our natural intercourse as commodities proves it. In the eyes of each other we are nothing but exchange values [*Tauschwerte*]. (23)

> In a similar way to these famous pages by Marx, "A Tune Just Like That" also lends its voice to musical commodities in general as a way of getting them to say and sing their second nature as fetishes: What we might call the musical self or the lyrical "I" of song would then be the voice of the commodity itself, in the midst of speaking about itself. This is certainly the phantasmagoria at work in "A Tune Just Like That": The musical commodity that the song is understands or recognizes itself; it enters into a relationship with another song, which is none other than another version of itself, and exchanges itself with it. And those who sing or whistle the tune are only able to meet one another and enter into a relationship to the extent that any given tune is already involved with itself, has already understood and recognized itself.

Benjamin is probably one of the few to have taken seriously the idea proposed ironically by Marx that a commodity might have a soul or a "point of view."

> If there were such a thing as a commodity-soul (a notion Marx occasionally mentions in jest), it would be the most empathetic ever encountered in the realm of souls, for it would be bound to see every individual as a buyer in whose hand and house it wants to nestle.[9]

For Benjamin, the psyche's identification with the thing exchanged on the market is one possible fate of the flâneur, who, "abandoned in the crowd," finds himself "in the same situation as the commodity" (31). The flâneur, Benjamin further writes, abandons himself to an "intoxication," which is that of the commodity itself, "immersed in a surging stream of customers" (31).

An intoxication of empathy, then, with the gaze or the hearing of things, an intoxication that Benjamin repeatedly attempts to grasp[10] and on which a song *feeds* in an exemplary way. In a fragment published posthumously, Benjamin mentions "the deepest temptation awakened by the refrain of a folk song," which is, he writes, "to throw the situation that is imagined here around one's shoulders, like a favorite old coat."[11] Like the flâneur with his boredom, this anamnesis of the song leads us to take on the perspective of things among themselves: The same fragment concludes that "folk art and kitsch," those spheres to which the hit essentially belongs, "allow us to look outward *from within objects*."[12]

Such would then be the veritable tale of "A Tune Just Like That," of that strolling, obsessive melody: the tale of an empathetic identification with the tune itself, insofar as it already lives from its encounter and its exchange with copies of itself. Whence, as a matter of fact, the touching and even very *moving boredom*, if one may say so, that it gives off as its most characteristic affect: It has the indolence of the flâneur, of the one who strolls dreaming in and of the place of commodities, from within their very souls as they await the eternal return of consummation.

"A Tune Just Like That," that sleepwalking melody that looks so bored as it passes from passerby to passerby, from her to him, and from you to me as we look at each other with surprise. Why are we surprised? Not because we're hearing something new (the tune, like the scene, couldn't be more banal), but because we're listening to something from the unheard-of place of a musical self that we've glimpsed only in passing and in our dreams: the place of the commodity itself.

Speaking of the Parisian arcades, those major commercial sites of flânerie to which Benjamin sought to devote his great unfinished book, Siegfried Kracauer, in his biography of Jacques Offenbach, wrote that they "display, as if on a stage, the marvelous possibilities of dreaming": They incarnate "that realm that was situated nowhere, over there, the place where songs are also born."[13]

If, according to certain of Benjamin's remarks, there may not have been any music proper to the arcades, song, when it takes on the form of the tune you whistle and hum, is nonetheless the perfect accompaniment to *flânerie* as it makes its way into the very heart of commodities.

With them, for them, *like them.*

That is to say: *just like that.*

Parole, Parole, Parole: The Desire for Self

Hits—"The Hit" by Boris Vian, for example—speak about hits. They speak about themselves, about their economy and their banality, perhaps even about the fantasies or indentificatory phantasmagorias, which, as commodities, they inspire. On their own, they say how they work and why they work on the market. For what reasons and for what causes they work, how it is they produce *themselves.*

We need to keep lending them an ear, a certain kind of ear.

As a matter of fact, we are getting ready to listen to a big hit that has crossed over many borders and will have a lot to tell us about the repetitive machines that successful songs so often are. This hit is a veritable masterpiece, and it's called "Parole, parole, parole" (1971), first sung in Italian by Mina, accompanied by the actor Alberto Lupo, and then covered in French by Dalida and Alain Delon.

"Words, words, words."

When Mina sings these words, the hit, through her voice, seems to want to speak the movement that carries it beyond itself in the paradoxical form of a perpetually unsatisfied desire: as if the hit, as a way of producing itself, were staging its desire for itself, that is to say its desire to be a pure song capable of attaining the end of words ("nothing but words"), capable of getting beyond them in its race toward a flight of lyricism. Between words and song, it's as if the hit were constantly taking itself up again on its path toward that absolute song that it is in the process of becoming. It is this structure or this self-desiring machine that is running after itself by digging a distance from itself into its very heart—by opening the gap between lyrics and song even further—it's this pursuit of self that we hear in an extremely pure form in "Parole, parole, parole."

For while Mina *sings* words ("words, only words"), the actor Alberto Lupo responds to her with *speech.* They divide the roles up between them, just as Dalida and Alain Delon do: She's the girl, he's the guy, as was the case in Boris Vian's "Tube"; but in this case, she will be Song and he will be Word. This is so much the case that the more one listens to the song, the more it appears to be an allegorical theater for two voices that stages the dialogue between the Sung and the Spoken in person, personified.

Imagine, then, that the ones in dialogue here are Speaking and Singing. Imagine that in the song itself, you are hearing a scene between Words and Song. Song would like to fly away by getting beyond her words and winning the race against them.

Here, then, is that scene. I will be transcribing its scenario line by line.

Words, in the person of Alberto Lupo, begin by saying to Song: My dear, *cara*, what is the matter with me tonight, *cosa mi succede stasera*, I see you and it's just like the first time, *ti guardo ed è come la prima volta*. Calling out to Song, addressing her in herself, Words, *her* words, tell her of a turmoil that is repeated and reinvented every time as if it were the first.

As for the Song found in the person of Mina, that is to say Song itself, the Sung of the song, she asks, repeating the question with ironic indifference: What are you, *cosa sei?*

Should we actually believe the Spoken of the song when he declares that he would like not to speak, *non vorrei parlare*, that he would prefer to say nothing, to abstain from answering the question, *cosa sei?*, that is incessantly troubling it? No. Because, incapable of remaining silent when faced with Song, he turns toward her and starts to *speak about her*. He tells her who she herself is: But you, you are love's sentence begun and never ending, *ma tu sei la frase d'amore cominciata e mai finita.*

We know, or we recognize, this scene of love or of lovers' quarrels. It is, as we shall see, the scene most widely and implicitly staged by many hits as a way of producing themselves as the songs they are. It is a scene where everything seems to happen as if, by letting her Words speak—by condemning them to speak over and over again, always ever more, to exhaust themselves in saying again and again who he and she are and what is going on between them—the Song in the song wanted to hear herself saying that she has always already started and will therefore never be able to stop. That the tiny machine she is knows no end, that she is even only that: a capacity for repetition that increases by being repeated.

As a way to say her desire for herself, a desire that carries her and constitutes her as the song she is, that keeps confirming her in her infinite affirmation of self, the Song in the song deploys all kinds of strategies and games of seduction addressed to the other, to that other in her that Words are. One could almost say that song shows herself off, that she doubles herself into Words and Song as a way of better claiming her place. And, by doing this, she ironizes about herself, she digs out within herself an ironic distance between self and self that turns her into an allegory of herself.[14]

You never change, *non cambi mai*, she repeats to her Words, to that Spoken that speaks of her within her: Try as you might, multiply your attempts with many forms and formulas, call me any name you like, use all the figures and all the tropes as they turn around and around in infinite and despairing equivalence, you'll never be able to, you will never be able to say what is happening this time yet again, just like the first time.

If Words seem to be forced to say what they are never able to say, is this not then so that the Sung can carry on by standing up to that other, the Spoken, which it is constantly denying as it moves on? You are my yesterday, my today, and my always, *tu sei il mio ieri, il mio oggi e il mio sempre*, the Spoken utters as best it can, interrupted by the Sung's ironic line: never, you will never really be able to, *proprio mai*.

But at this point, we're nearing the refrain. The first couplet is almost ready to end when the Spoken starts things up again: You are my worry, he says, *inquietudine*; you are my intranquility; you are the movement, concern, or desire that moves me and sets me in motion, that gets me started and that shatters me. We are here at the threshold of that lyrical flight that will furnish the ritornello of the refrain, a veritable hit within the hit that will finish off the Spoken with the blow of a *Caramelle, non ne voglio più* (by which one should understand: I don't want any more of these little candies, of these saccharine sentimentalities, of these caramelized ornaments that you keep offering). And it's at this point, at this threshold, just as Song is getting ready to take off, that it gives itself away and takes flight: Now, Mina sings, you can always try, *adesso ormai ci puoi tentare*; you can say whatever you want; go ahead, yeah, come on, *dai*, call me your torment, while you're at it, *chiamami tormento dai, già che si sei*. Translated, this means: Tell me, or rather, let me tell myself in myself and through you, this torment that I am. Or, better still: this great torment, this *tormentone*, as Italians say to mean, quite precisely, a hit, this obsessive melody that torments us and that I myself am pursuing here, I, the Sung of the song.

Here, at the point where the refrain is just around the corner, at the moment when the sung par excellence is just about to rise, words and figures no longer matter; any image or any metaphor is just as good as any other when faced with the decisive blow that is getting ready to reduce the Spoken to the most powerless banality. As it happens, and as if out of despair, Alberto Lupo, who is more laughable than ever in his role as a lyricist personifying Words, declares: You are like the wind that brings the violins and roses, *tu sei come il vento che porta i violini e le rose.* How sappy he is, that poor Spoken guy, how miserable he seems next to Song, who is getting ready to unfold her wings into the lyricism of the refrain.

Yet the decisive blow dealt to Words is also a theatrical bluff. For out of the absolute banality of the most mediocre and overcooked poetic brainwave, out of those violins and roses so overused and bleached out in their sentimentality, there emerges for the first time, *come la prima volta*, the performative force of these worn-out words. *Violini*, says the Spoken, and, as if by magic, that word performatively calls into existence the aforementioned violins, which are immediately heard emerging from the orchestra: The Spoken does what it names; it creates it. Or perhaps we should say that it is Song; it is the flight of the refrain that saves words by taking them away, which takes them up again at the very moment they seemed to be definitively emptied out.

The refrain is the moment when the song should become the Song it is trying to be, among the shadows it casts and the silhouettes it breathes into the Spoken on this theatrical stage of its own becoming. A stage where it acts itself out for itself. this scene of love or of lovers' quarrels, a scene of auto-affection, as a way of *producing itself*, in itself and for itself.

So there she is on her way, the Song within the song; there she is taking flight into the lyricism of that coming ritornello, sovereign in her affirmation of herself: No more saccharine words, she sings, *caramelle, non ne voglio più*, and the roses and the violins, you can go tell them to someone else, *le rose e i violini questa sera raccontali a un'altra*; I can listen to them when and if I want to, *li posso sentire quando la cosa mi va se mi va.*

Confronted with this sovereign auto-positioning of the Song within the song, where and when she wants to, the Spoken gives up: I don't understand you, he says, *non ti capisco*; I don't get you any more; you escape me; you are what escapes yourself in us. The Spoken becomes a supplication, a prayer: One more word, *una parola ancora.* But, increasingly, the Spoken loses itself in the Song's refrain as it repeats: Words, words, words, *parole, parole, parole.* Listen to me, moans the Spoken, *ascoltami*; I beg you; *ti prego*; I swear to you; *io ti giuro.* He begs Song to give him the opportunity for more performative promises, while sovereign Song gets carried away into the sublime and indifferent repetition of the word *word*, emptied out and exhausted. *Parole, soltanto parole*, sings Mina, who is sovereign here. Words, nothing but words, the word *word* sung seven times: *Parole, parole, parole, parole, parole, soltanto parole, parole.*

It looks as if the race is won and as if words have been surpassed. As if the Song in the song, the Hit in the hit has ended up finding itself, overcoming the distance that separated it from itself, satisfying its desire for itself in the auto-affective jouissance of the refrain's flight of lyricism.

And yet.

And yet, one further theatrical bluff intervenes with the victorious repetition of this final blow to Saying. For at the very moment that the refrain concludes by wearing words out by repeating them, the last word, the final word of the song as it empties out words, is this one, which reaffirms and starts the race all over again as it takes up the course or discourse of an impossible dialogue: *parole, soltanto parole, parole tra noi*, words, only words, words between us. This is the last word—and everything begins again.

Between us, yes. Between us, says the Song of the song to its Words, between us there are only words. Between me who sings (to) you and you who speaks (to) me, between me who speaks (to) me through you and me who looks for myself as song, there is nothing but that, words, *parole, parole.* The difference—that which is between in this between-us, between myself and myself—is the word.

And that is why everything starts up and repeats again, like the very destiny of a hit: This is my destiny, says Saying in the person of Alberto Lupo, *ecco il mio destino*, speaking to you, speaking to you as if for the first time, *parlarti, parlarti come la prima volta.*

Repetition, or the Ordeal of Enthusiasm

The self-desiring structure that "Parole, parole, parole" has just sung for us—in which the hit stages itself as being in search of itself, with and beyond words, to ensure that it is incessantly reproduced and reborn, always starting up again each time like the first time—can be found in somewhat less pure forms in many successful songs.

Two examples among many others.

I am listening to "Satisfaction," to Mick Jagger's voice as it sings: "I can't get no satisfaction/'Cause I try and I try and I try and I try,/I can't get no, I can't get no . . ." Who is this "*I*"? Who is this musical self? Who is this fictional subject that gives voice to his unsatisfied desire? It may well be, once again, that it is the hit itself. That it is this successful 1965 song by the Stones that says and has continuously said from the moment it was released: I cannot find satisfaction; I try all the time; I've really tried, but I just can't do it. As if the song itself, then, were there complaining about the guy on the radio who just keeps on talking, ("that man comes on the radio/And he's tellin' me more and more"), of the guy who talks about "some useless information/Supposed to fire my imagination." This means that "Satisfaction" has become a kind of allegory of the song that it is, a song that would say that no, no, no, as long as it keeps speaking, as long as something or someone speaks in me, I am not satisfied: "I can't get no, oh, no no no,/ . . . that's what I say,/I can't get no satisfaction."

In the same way, when Stevie Wonder sings "Isn't She Lovely" in 1976, isn't he really, above and beyond the apparent pretext of the birth of his daughter Aisha, celebrating his song itself? "Isn't she lovely?" he wonders, "isn't she wonderful, isn't she precious, less than one minute old?" And so on and so forth ad infinitum, with, in the background, a childish *wordless* babbling that seems to offer a figure for the pure song to be attained through incessant births and rebirths.

But instead of listing the innumerable examples—there are so many hits that are each very similar and all very different—we must instead ask ourselves: So what exactly is a hit? Is it simply, as Boris Vian maintained, "a song destined to 'be a success'?"

One obvious possibility would be to turn to statistics, to try to find out how many copies of "Parole, parole, parole" or “Un air comme ça” were sold and then to figure out how many times the song will have been repeated and what this might mean for the odds that it will come to haunt people’s memories. Here, though, I will avoid the criterion of quantifiable numbers. I do this not only to preserve the admirable possibility Rodolphe Burger once described for me—he once told me that one of the ambitions of his group Kat Onoma was to create “underground hits”—but also because a criterion like this will only be able to indicate one among the many aspects of a hit: the number of copies it has sold.

At the risk of disappointing anyone looking for a recipe for how to put hits out on the market or for identifying them with certainty before they are released,[15] my attempt will rather be to trace out a *hitology*, a logic of the hit capable of accounting for an economy of success without reducing it to statistics, for success does not simply happen, or not happen, to a song once it has been released onto the market of mass distribution.

We have already begun to make out the logic of the hit in “Un air comme ça” and “Parole, parole, parole.” Boris Vian’s song sang of the encounter between a girl and a guy—a banal, interchangeable encounter that presents itself as the encounter of musical commodities among themselves and that operates according to the phantasmagoria of the fetish analyzed first by Marx and then by Benjamin. In contrast, Mina’s hit, with its staging of self-desiring love, claimed to want to get beyond the well-worn banality of its words to fly away to a space of pure lyricism where it would each time be capable of finding the unique and singular flavor of the first time once again.

What is unique and what is cliché, the incomparable and the interchangeable, the psyche and the market: This may well be the big story behind hits. But in order to better understand how they are able to tie the apparently incompatible characteristics of banality and singularity together in an unprecedented knot, we must now turn to one of the most fascinating ways of thinking about that quintessential structure of song: repetition. We must, in other words, take the apparent detour that is actually not one at all and read Kierkegaard's great little book or philosophical novel: *Repetition.*[16]

As its subtitle indicates, *Repetition* is an *Essay in Experimental Psychology.* It is also a great story, whose protagonists are the narrator, Constantin Constantius, and a "young man" subject to the tribulations of romantic passion, to the pains of eros, in short, to love—which is also a way of relating to repetition.

Even if it does not directly treat the question of song, *Repetition* nonetheless evokes it several times, either as a metaphor for obsession[17] or else literally, when the narrator cites a "popular song." Constantin Constantius (whose name is itself a repetition) does in fact cite one particular song that speaks of an unhappy, wounded love for a young woman who has entered into a convent, and he cites it to support his conviction that in love, repetition can be neither expected nor predicted, in short, that it cannot be the object of any knowledge or any system.

> How can one get such a foolish idea, and, still more foolishly, how can one want to make a principle of it. My young friend thought: Let it pass—and he thereby would have been far better off than if he had wanted to begin with repetition. Then he probably would have gained the beloved again in the same way as the lover in the folk

song who wanted repetition, as the nun with shorn hair and pale lips. (174)

Popular song thus illustrates the paradox of repetition that the entire book is trying to explain: When repetition is possible, when it can be thought through or programmed as possible *in principle*, then it is impossible and will not occur; but, as we will see with the example of Job, when it is impossible, when it seems to be out of the question, when nothing allows you to expect or hope for it, then, *perhaps*, repetition will occur in spite of it all.

Possible as impossible and impossible as possible: We will now attempt to approach this mystery in order to try to understand something about the strange *singularity of the cliché*, of that *unique experience of repetition* that hits propose to us or impose on us.

It is in fact Job, the biblical character with whom the young man identifies, who will embody the *impossible possibility* of repetition. Because it is he who "gives birth to the category of the 'ordeal'" (210).

What exactly is this?

Job, as is well known, endures the worst ordeals God sends his way. And the final ordeal, the test of tests, is that he is even refused the capacity of finding a reason or explanation for them, of inscribing them into an economy of punishment or regret. In this hyperbolic sense, the ordeal is beyond any calculation and any principle of *possible* restitution or reparation. It is at this precise point, at the end of an ordeal that is impossible because unthinkable, that repetition happens for Job, as the young man explains in his January 13 letter to the narrator.

> This is called a repetition. . . . When did it occur for Job? When every *thinkable* human certainty and probability were impossible. Bit by bit he loses everything, and hope thereby gradually vanishes, inasmuch as actuality, far from being placated, rather lodges stronger and stronger allegations against him. . . . His friends . . . know but one way out, that by submitting to the punishment he may dare to hope for a repetition to the point of overflowing. Job will not have it. (212–13)

If this is then the experience of the impossible named by the Kierkegaardian categories of ordeal and repetition, this does not make them any more extractable from the thread of the narrative that *Repetition* is. We must therefore briefly trace out this narrative to situate the moment when, faced with a popular show, in a vaudeville theater, the spectator also becomes a kind of Job who is no longer confronted with the misfortunes that befall him but with the cliché, with the commonplace, with that iterability that is the very material of our hits and from which, *perhaps*, what the narrator calls "the Unique" will emerge.

It so happens that *Repetition* is divided into two main sections, and that the second section repeats the title of the work: "Repetition."

Interspersed with theoretical remarks on repetition, the first section contains narrative episodes: first the young man's love story, then a trip to Berlin over the course of which Constantin Constantius will attempt to relive his past experiences at the theater by going to see the popular vaudeville that he had loved. Like the first section, the second section is framed by general considerations about repetition, and it takes up the young man's story yet again, this time in the form of letters that weave his narrative in with the biblical figure of Job. The book ends with an epilogue to the reader.

Without being able to follow along the many detours of this masterly philosophical novel and its incredibly inventive structure, let me simply say that it is constructed in a "tubular"[18] fashion, in other words through a network of interlocking narrative tubes or canalizations, with all the risks this implies for saturation at the joints and different branches of the pipes.

This is what brings the reader, who has been canalized up to the end of the first section, right up to the end of this first narrative conduit, to the sense and experience of a stagnation, perhaps even to a veritable clog in the conduct or flow of the story, which seems not to want to start up again, to have to stop at the threshold of the repetition of the title, *Repetition*, at that point where the course of the story might get blocked up.

> The journey is not worth the trouble, for one need not stir from the spot to be convinced that there is no repetition. No, one sits calmly in one's living room; when all is vanity and passes away. . . . Travel on, you fugitive river! . . . for you want only to flow along and lose yourself in the sea, which is never filled! . . . Move on, you drama of existence, where life is not given again any more than money is! . . .

> **Repetition**

> Some time went by. My servant, like a housewifely Eve, had remedied his earlier wrongdoing. A monotonous and unvarying order was established in my whole economy . . . I had convinced myself that there is no repetition,

it nevertheless is always certain and true that by being inflexible and also by dulling one's powers of observation a person can achieve a sameness that has a far more anesthetic power than the most whimsical amusements. . . . In the excavation of Herculaneum and Pompeii, everything was found in its place just as the respective owners left it. If I had lived at that time, the archeologists, perhaps to their amazement, would have come upon a man who walked with measured pace up and down the floor. (175–79)

This paralysis of a narrator who is convinced of the impossibility of any kind of repetition, his fossil-like clotting in the midst of the river of existence, is what paradoxically allows us to *pass* into the second narrative conduit, the *Repetition* inside *Repetition* that will lead us straight to Job.

Somewhat like the young man reading the Book of Job, the reader of *Repetition* undergoes here an experience of the impossibility of repetition and of the overall stagnation of the situation. Yet it is at the very moment when any new departure seems impossible that the event nonetheless takes place: "One day a letter arrived from my young friend," writes the narrator, who then takes us little by little into the correspondence with the young man, where, under the sign of Job, the only veritable repetition will emerge.

In short, the reader, too, will have been put through a kind of ordeal: *In spite of it all*, he or she goes through the point where reading itself seemed to be definitively clogged. And with even less recourse to hope or knowledge, given that the narrator has done everything to have the reader believe that repetition is impossible. That life is not given again, any more than is a reading or a listening.[19]

* * *

Repetition happens, then, in *Repetition*, at the very moment that we no longer believe in it at all. And with good reason: The trip to Berlin that the narrator had undertaken to "test the possibility and meaning of repetition" (150), the trip that brought him back to the Königstädter Theater to see a play whose memory was so strong in him—this test, then, had ended in failure: "I endured it for half an hour and then left the theater, thinking: There is no repetition at all" (169).

So what is it that actually happened in that theater?

In spite of the apparent failure, it is worth our while to linger here for a moment in the company of Constantin, for it is here in this popular burlesque theater where "farces" were acted out that the narrator will have encountered the repetition of cliché, of the commonplace. It is through the experience of the cliché that what we were least expecting emerges—the unique and the singular.

On the verge of describing the scene of the farce and its actors, Constantin compares it to "a Nuremberg print" (158)—in reference to the engravings produced in series in that town starting in 1796, often as illustrations for popular songs. Contrasting farce with the "perfection" of tragedy or comedy, Constantin affirms that the same is true for the Nuremberg image, which he compares to "the painting of a consummate art." What in effect do we encounter in this kind of popular cliché? This, for example:

> There one sees a landscape depicting a rural area in general. This abstraction cannot be artistically executed. Therefore the whole thing is achieved by contrast, namely, by an accidental concretion. And yet I ask everyone if from such a landscape he does not get the impression of a rural area in general, and if this category had not stayed with him

> from childhood. In the days of childhood, we had such enormous categories that they now almost make us dizzy, we clipped out of a piece of paper a man and a woman who were man and woman in general in a more rigorous sense than Adam and Eve were. . . . [A] print like that produces an indescribable effect, since we do not know whether to laugh or cry, and the whole effect depends upon the observer's mood. (158)

Adam and Eve cut out of paper like a girl and a guy in general: The dizzying generality of the commonplace that comes from its banality (from the interchangeable character of its subject "taken up by chance") is also, quite precisely, that of farce, whose effect, says Constantin, "depends largely on the spontaneity and creative activity of the spectator" (159, translation modified). This is why, according to a paradoxical and yet extremely refined logic, Constantin concludes from this that the spectator of farce becomes *extraordinary* to the precise extent that what is presented to him comes from the most well-worn ordinariness. Confronted with the vertigo of the general that arises from the cliché, there is no longer any rule that remains valid; nothing regulates the spectator's attitude or judgment, and nothing can program them or make them certain in advance.

> A proper theater public generally has a certain restricted earnestness; it wishes to be . . . ennobled and educated in the theater. It wishes to have had—or at least fancies that it has had—a rare artistic enjoyment; it wishes, as soon as it has read the poster, to be able to know in advance what is going to happen that evening. Such unanimity cannot be found at a farce, for the same farce can produce very different impressions, and, strangely enough, it

> may so happen that the one time it made the least impression it was performed best. Thus a person cannot rely on his neighbor and the man across the street and statements in the newspaper to determine whether he has enjoyed himself or not. The individual has to decide that matter for himself. . . . [I]n a farce all of the characters are portrayed according to the abstract criterion "in general." Situation, action, the lines—everything is according to this criterion. Therefore one can just as well be made sad as ecstatic from laughter. . . . Therefore, the viewer must be self-active. (159–60)

In short, confronted with the commonplace of the farce or of the Nuremberg image, aesthetic norms are obliterated. And everyone, *each one*, becomes unique, in other words finds himself, or herself, faced with a test of himself, or herself, as if it were a question of gambling, of putting everything on the line in a game of chance: "For a cultured person, seeing a farce is similar to playing the lottery, except that one does not have the annoyance of winning money" (159).

This is, then, in Constantin's aesthetic experience, the ordeal of farce, which also brings up an impossible repetition, a repetition that is possible as impossible. This is the very repetition that hits, which are also sonorous stereotypes, ask us to consider along the lines of that strange structure of theirs in which the cliché, in its interchangeable banality, is nonetheless *unique every time for each one of us.*

And yet, one may object, precisely by returning to see a farce he had so treasured, Constantin convinced himself that repetition is impossible ("and I left the theater thinking: 'There no repetition at all' " [169]).

Well, yes, in fact, there is. As is the case with hits, with our refrains so worn out that we can't stand to hear them again, the moment we are expecting it the least is the moment when we are seized by them in our deepest depths. It's once nothing seems possible any more that we listen to them and they come by chance to unearth in us what we keep most secret: a past moment, happy time, or a shameful emotion or impulse that belongs only to us.

And it may well be that they, too, do this by staging their own *tubular* form: Listening to them tell of the test to which they are putting themselves and their own banality, hearing a refrain rise like the wind in the middle of the most idiotic old song, like the reader of *Repetition* who experiences the passage by choking up, we sing with them, in them, we hum the impossibility of what will nonetheless, perhaps, happen—the singular possibility of an incomparable ravishment.

Such is the obstructing enthusiasm [*engouement*] of hits and for hits.[20]

Each time unique, in the impossible.

CHAPTER 3 The Filmography of Hits

I Have Come to Tell You . . .: Same Old Song

Having followed Kierkegaard to a popular theater, we must now go to the movies.

Not only because, as we have seen, hits are quite their own kind of production,[1] with their love scenes and self-desiring scenes; not only because, listening to them, we project all kinds of scenarios onto the girl and the guy and the infinite variations of their encounters and separations. But in particular because at some of its best moments, film allows us to think about the logic of hits we are investigating. It shows it to us, literally, at work. And it does so by articulating the banal with the singular and the market with the psyche in a particularly powerful way.

Films that deal with hits are nonetheless few and far between. It is really in a more indirect way that the cinema, in general, speaks of songs by using them as one among several of its means. This in no way stops the cinema—as we will see in certain scenes by Fritz Lang or Hitchcock—from *thinking* hits.

There is, however, at least one film that, in a magnificent way, presents itself as a veritable treatise on hitology: *Same*

Old Song (*On connaît la chanson*) by Alain Resnais (1997). It is the starting point for this brief consideration of the filmography of earworms.

Before we can really pay close attention to several scenes in *Same Old Song* in which the characters are ventriloquized by the hits that obsess us all, we must take the time to consider a premise. Before watching and listening, we must first read the one who could have been (though it is not actually the case) the author of the screenplay, so much does his writing seem to analyze in advance what happens to the musically obsessed characters that we observe in Resnais's film.

I'm speaking of Theodor Reik, one of Freud's close and faithful disciples, who, unlike so many other psychoanalysts, tried to think about the place of music in unconscious mechanisms.

In 1953, in a probably unconscious parody of the subtitle of Kierkegaard's *Repetition* (*An Essay in Experimental Psychology*), Reik wrote a remarkable work subtitled *Psychoanalytical Experiences in Life and Music.* I have read and reread this essay many times, and I am constantly going back to reading it, as if it might explain the unexplainable to me—the phenomenon of the "obsessive melody," as the French translation of Reik's book would have it. My translation of Reik's title would emphasize its ghostliness. Reik, at any rate, titled his book *The Haunting Melody.*[2]

The melody that interests Reik acts, then, like a ghost that has come to haunt us. Or like a worm, a virus of the ear that keeps reproducing itself in us. To bring some obstructive enthusiasm into our heart of hearts: traffic jams, in other words, in the movement at the heart of our psyche (isn't that what obsession is?); but also bursts of enthusiasm, lyrical flights of incomparable force and emotion.

Reik gives a striking example of this kind of obstructive enthusiasm when he recounts his analysis of one of his patients named Cecily (who shares her name with the patron saint of musicians) in whom an "obsessional idea" had emerged whose source was unclear to her: "She did not know why she was now convinced that the journey to India was a necessary premise for having a baby" (34).

It so happens that the mental block brought on by the incomprehensible idée fixe, which is constantly coming back with greater and greater strength, affects not only Cecily, but also the analysis itself, that is to say the analyst, Reik, who admits that he feels "helpless." He, too, experiences a traffic jam in the movement of the cure, which walks in place without moving forward because something is saturated.

This is the moment when a ghostly melody intervenes, a tune by Mendelssohn that suddenly emerges among the associations of the listening analyst and which will suddenly untie the knot or unblock what the obsessive fixation had stopped up.

> While I listened to this patient who was possessed by that mysterious idea, the tune of Mendelssohn's *Auf Flügeln des Gesanges* came clearly to my mind. . . . I was very surprised when the quietly floating and tender melody of Mendelssohn's *lied* emerged, but I had learned to pay attention to such intercurrent thoughts during analytic sessions. My astonishment lasted only a second, and then the clear recognition of the origin of Cecily's obsessive thought emerged.

What is it then that happened thanks to the impromptu emergence of this tune called "On the Wings of Song"? The tune, says Reik, had been familiar to him "since early childhood."

> My mother sang that *lied* many times, and although I did not then understand all the text I realized that it was a love song, full of tenderness and longing. I knew that India was a faraway country, and an aunt of mine had once told me that the stork brought babies from there. . . . The process by which the analytic understanding of Cecily's idea was reached can be sketched in the following manner. While I listened to her, there must have been an unconscious preknowledge that some infantile notion connected with babies and India was at the roots of her thought. Her speaking of a plane trip to that country brought the word and perhaps the image: airplane . . . wings, to my mind. The tune *Auf Flügeln des Gesanges* that occurred to me is determined by the thought link of *Flügeln* (wings). . . . Instead of the conscious thought that I believed as a child the stork brought babies from India—the patient must also have thought babies were brought from there—the memory of Mendelssohn's song appeared. A second later the recognition of Cecily's idea was clearly in my mind. With the tune and its text the unconscious guess stepped over the threshold of conscious perception. (36–37)

So the melody appeared thanks to the metonymy of the trip to India as wings: It represents the obsessive idea and musically incarnates the fixation's consistency and strength. But it is also what, almost at the same time, unblocks or unstops the saturation, thus preparing a resolving fluidification that looks a lot like a burst of enthusiasm, like a flight on the wings of song, in short, an obstructive enthusiasm within the progress of the cure.

In addition to this kind of always interesting case analysis, the explicit and declared object of Reik's study is to look for the *meaning* of these old saws that besiege us by interrupting the course of life. "What does it mean," he wonders on the first page of the book, "when some tune follows you, occurs to you again and again so that it becomes a haunting melody?" A little further on, he asks himself:

> What does it mean when a melody occurs to you in the middle of thoughts of a quite different kind, when your mind is occupied with rational considerations and aim-directed thoughts? (7)

Yet, in terms of a musico-psychological inquiry into meaning, Reik's investigation will soon find itself at an impasse. In the great romantic tradition of absolute music, Reik believes that the melody as such is "a message which everybody understands, but nobody can translate" (7). And yet, what he constantly does is, quite precisely, to translate, to inscribe music in a *signifying* discourse. When he writes, for example, that "in the flow of free associations, snatches of tunes are interspersed at certain significant points" (10), it is clear that meaning and signification reside not in music, but in the places that the implicit discourse of free association makes for it. Whether it is already there or still lacking—because it is hidden in the interstices of the conscious or unconscious material—meaning seems for Reik to be discursive. And, as it happens, each of his—extremely sensitive and elaborate—analyses of the phenomenon of musical ghosts and each one of his case studies ends with the reduction, or translation, of melody into a signifying discourse, into "phrases" or "words." Because it is almost always the *lyrics* to the songs that Reik investigates, sometimes even connecting a hidden text to the music drawn from contextual or biographical elements.[3]

Yet Reik seems to worry about this: "It must make a difference," he confides, "whether a sentence from a speech, a line from a poem or a tune emerges in your train of thoughts" (10). Reik seems to skirt around a difference he is not able to grasp but which nonetheless haunts him: What is proper to music? What is there that is properly musical or *musically obsessive* in haunting melodies?

I would like to argue that what is at stake here is not a difference in meaning, but a difference in *strength*. What music has that is (relatively) proper to it would be not its own meaning, but its capacity as a snag and a stroke of luck (*d'accroc et de raccroc*) that makes its interruptions so irruptive and eruptive. When it comes down to it, beyond the infinite forms of discourse Reik rightly or wrongly attributes to the haunting melodies he studies, what these musical ghosts have in common is the strength of their emergence. Reik always describes it eloquently: Such and such a *lied*, he recounts, "appeared surprisingly in the middle of a conversation or following a train of thought which had not the slightest perceptible connection with the text of the song" (40); "tunes," he notes elsewhere, "invade and usurp the mental sphere against resistance, and occupy its realm for hours and sometimes for days" (166); a melody that has been haunting him for several days, he confides, "came like an unannounced guest one has once known, but whose name one has forgotten" (181).

I could multiply these quotations where Reik, without making it his primary preoccupation, and almost in an aside, names the singular strength of this reiterated irruption, which, as far as music is concerned, *makes the difference.* I would propose that we think of this strength, or rather this difference of strength, as something that could be called *reiterruption.* The word marks the fact that, before even saying anything at all, before even fulfilling its expectation or its suspension of meaning, an earworm (another possible translation for Reik's "haunting melody") is already speaking of its ghostly round trip: Above all else, it says—with or without words but on the wings of song—that it obsessively comes and goes.

What Reik perhaps does not see in his quest to discover the unconscious or hidden meaning transmitted by haunting melodies is shown in an exemplary way in Gainsbourg's song "Je suis venu te dire que je m'en vais" ("I Have Come to Tell You That I'm Leaving") as it appears in Resnais's film.

In effect, in each of its brief appearances in *Same Old Song,* this hit seems to take possession of Claude, one of the film's characters, played by Pierre Arditi. It seems to lend itself to his thoughts, to carry them and give them a form that is both ephemeral and lasting: reiterable, but each time charged with a singularly intense affect.

Agnès Jaoui, one of the screenplay writers, compares refrains like this to "proverbs." Like "the sun always comes out after the rain" or "you have to take things easy." And she adds that they are like "readymade ideas, commonplaces that summarize an emotion and, at the same time, cheapen it."[4] Indeed, thanks to the repetition that seems to have always inhabited it, the hit is all the more hospitable to any and all emotional ghosts to the extent that it offers them *whatever* a kind of a place, one that has already been visited and revisited to the point that it has properly become a *common*place. But the Kierkegaardian paradox, as we have seen, is that the affect seems to nourish its intensification with its very impoverishment, as if it were exasperated not by *the fact that* it is becoming whatever, but *within* that very becoming.

"I Have Come to Tell You That I'm Leaving" comes up four times in the film, at variable intervals and for various lengths of time. (1) Claude gets out of the car and kisses the woman he loves, and the song begins to resound within him as he turns to go to the apartment where his wife Odile (Sabine Azéma) is having a housewarming party; will he tell her, as the refrain is whispering it into his ear, that he wants to leave her? (2) Odile and her guests are wondering where Claude is, while we briefly see him walking down the street repeating Gainsbourg's words, as if he had finally made his decision. (3) Claude, pensive in the midst of people who had come for the party, dreams wide awake of his farewell scene with Odile. (4) Claude comes up to finally say the decisive words but is interrupted by Odile's despair. She has just discovered the trick Marc (Lambert Wilson), the real estate agent who sold her the apartment, has played on her.

Each time, then, that "I Have Come to Tell You That I'm Leaving" comes to Claude's mind, in each one of these reiterruptions, or musical comings and goings, it is a question of moving from music to life. Gainsbourg's voice starts to sing in Claude. In vain, Claude tries to take up the words that first began to resound within him in the form of a melody, but this time he wants to say them, to pronounce and address them with all of their performative value. Claude thus attempts to give an *effect* to these words come to take possession of him; he would like to make them effective and *do* something with them. He would like for life to be like music. Yet whether it is spoken or sung, the song disappears each time as quickly as it had appeared. The song that brings Claude the words he would like to make his own—words that name his desire to separate from Odile—almost just as quickly takes them away. It takes them away from him by going away.

The song, then, circulates from the sung to the spoken, from the spoken to the sung, from one moment to another, from one scene to another, from music to life; it leaves its musical world to come take hold of a character that it then leaves to return to the place it had come from. Arrival and return. This is the round trip of the refrain, of the tune, which in the final analysis seems to be talking above all about itself and about its repeated visits or visitations when it utters: "I have come to tell you that I'm leaving."[5]

This hit by Gainsbourg also speaks the law of all the other hits that come and go in *Same Old Song* by ventriloquizing each of the characters in turn. "Me," each of the old saws seems to say each time they emerge in the film, "I have come to immediately go away." This is in fact how Resnais describes them: "The songs we used," he explains, "are the ones that came to us naturally, through an association of ideas. Most of the extracts are extremely short, sometimes cut right in the middle, something that corresponds to the way thought proceeds (it is rare that one remembers all of a chorus to a song, and even rarer to remember all of the verses)."

It is indeed the case that in *Same Old Song*, so many songs that we all know come and go and, like Gainsbourg's, speak both about themselves—about their comings and goings from reemergence to oblivion—and about life, which is also made up of repetition, snags, and strokes of luck. There is, for example, Julien Clerc's voice as it sings "It's Nothing": "You know it well," he sings, "they go away like boats and then suddenly, it all comes back."[6] For here, songs are like those "walnut husks" he mentions in the same lines: They come and go, just as the tide rises and falls, with the association of ideas. Claude François says the same thing when he belts out his "Popular Song ("It goes away and then comes back, made up of the smallest things")[7]. It is also what Michel Sardou sings through the mouth of the moving character played by André Dussolier: "This impression of déjà-vu, of having already gone through this; I am sure I already heard this song before tonight."[8] The title of the song, "Déjà-vu," is emblematic: as if the song itself bore the memory—and hence the prophecy—of its own repetition.[9]

Like a phone call, every time a song rings and then hangs up, every time the song calls back, it seems to have always already called. And many songs describe this. They articulate the fact that they proceed *through lucky breaks,*[10] that is through the improbable and unexpected repetition of good or bad luck. They say what they are doing: They sing the fact that they are emerging or reemerging by interrupting the normal course of life even as they, too, allow themselves to be interrupted by it. Like ghosts, these melodies come to torment the characters, hits which, as the Italians so aptly put it, are *tormentoni*: great tormentors, old saws that inhabit and haunt the life of the ones they besiege by promising them a continual return.

In another sequence of *Same Old Song*, Camille (Agnès Jaoui) is telling her sister Odile about the love affair she's having with Marc. Odile is very happy about it, but also concerned to know if Camille is nonetheless able to think about her dissertation. "Tell me, though, I hope you aren't forgetting to work?" she asks her. And Camille's answer takes the form of a song: Edith Piaf singing *J'm'en fous pas mal* ("I Don't Give a Damn"): "Anything can happen to me/I don't give a damn./I have my lover who is mine,/It may well be banal."[11] It's as if Camille, sitting on the sofa in the living room next to her sister, were quietly seized by Piaf's voice, which makes her go on to say: "There are his arms that embrace me,/There is his body, soft and warm."[12] Yet between these two phrases, the scene changes even as the song goes on. It is no longer the same place and no longer the same time. This time, we see Odile's husband, Claude, who is in bed, listening to Piaf on the radio. He closes his eyes to dream: Hearing the same song, he thinks of the other woman, the one he loves. From one character to another (from Camille to Claude), moving from one scene to another, this is how the song gets around; it passes over the interruption of the editor's cut and ends up itself being interrupted by a gesture from Odile, who simply turns the radio off. First appearing in the soundtrack, then passing into the reduced space of the transistor radio (a kind of space within the space of the film), the song ends up disappearing as abruptly as it had appeared.

Interrupting, being interrupted: Such is the condition for the song's circulation, its ability to switch gears, in a way, by moving onto or into life. So that it can be tied to life, articulated in it, mixed up with it.

Following along the humming detours of the characters in *Same Old Song*, who seem to be perfect illustrations of Reik's psychoanalytic and musically obsessed stories, following alongside Odile, Claude, Camille, and the others, who could all be patients of Reik offering him "cases" to study, hits indeed appear as working toward the reiterruption about which so many songs are already singing when they tell us: "I have come to tell you that I'm leaving."

The Market and the Psyche: Fritz Lang's M

For Claude and for the other characters in *Same Old Song,* as well as for the musically obsessed patients analyzed by Reik, hits or earworms, because they speak in anticipation of their comings and goings between the unconscious and the conscious, are guided by a pure structure of confession: First of all, they give voice to the very movement of confession, and without it needing to have any kind of content: They are the gesture that consists in confessing something without the avowal's having yet crystallized into any particular avowal. *I came to tell you . . . ,* they say, without yet saying anything at all: I came to tell you that there is something to say, especially since I'm going away, so that I can come back to tell you over and over again that there is still something to say.

In this sense, earworms share certain characteristics with what Reik, in another essay, calls the *compulsion to confess.*[13] (And, in fact, in French slang, a *tube* is also, if not quite a confession, than at least a clue, a confidential bit of information. In other words, a *tip* [*un tuyau*]).

Nothing can prove that Boris Vian, when he initiated the musical use of the word, had this sense in mind, even though his first novel (*J'irai cracher sur vos tombes* [I will go spit on your graves], 1946) was actually found at a crime scene open to the page describing a strangulation, a fact that contributed to his being judged guilty of offending public decency in 1950. One thing, however, is certain: The history of hits is intertwined with criminology, police investigations, and other tales of detectives on the lookout for clues, evidence, and confessions.

This can be observed in an exemplary way in Fritz Lang's *M* (1931). M, the pedophile criminal magnificently portrayed by Peter Lorre, whispers a famous tune from Grieg's *Peer Gynt* ("In the Hall of the Mountain King") every time he is getting ready to throw himself at one of his young victims.[14]

Yet the film already opens with a song: a little nursery rhyme being recited by children standing in a circle in the inner courtyard of a building: "Wait, wait just a minute, soon the dark man will come to you" (*Warte, warte nur ein Weilchen, bald kommt der schwarze Mann zu dir*). A worried mother who is in the midst of hanging her wash on the balcony cries out to them: "You shouldn't be singing that damn song." But as soon as she disappears, the children take up their refrain again. We then see the mother carrying the wash up to the next floor and complaining about the horrible refrain to her neighbor, who tells her that "as long as we hear them singing it, at least we know that they're there."[15]

This same neighbor—who will soon be revealed to be the mother of the first victim—is making lunch for her daughter while waiting for her to come home. The film cuts from shots showing the mother's tenderly smiling face to the vision of the daughter leaving school and going along her way, bouncing her ball first on the sidewalk and then against a poster posted on a column: On the poster, one can read the promise of a 10,000-mark reward for the identification of the murderer at loose in the city. As round as the zeroes of the announced sum, the ball keeps hitting the poster over and over again until the shadow of a man sporting a hat is also projected against it, as if against a screen. "You have a nice ball," he says to the child. "What's your name?" "Elsie Beckmann," she answers. After a sequence that shows the waiting mother's increasing concern, the camera films the man in the hat from behind as he buys a balloon from a blind vendor (*Blind* is written across the board hanging around his neck) to give it to little Elsie. He has just begun to sound the fateful tune from *Peer Gynt*, whistling it in a distracted way. A tune *just like that.*

After other images of the mother's anxious waiting, after her cries of despair ("Elsie! Elsie!") echo into the void, there is a silence that accompanies the next two shots: first the ball rolling in the grass; then the balloon, twisted into the shape of a child's silhouette, flies away, bumping up against poles and electric lines. The image fades to darkness from which we hear emerge the ghostly voice of a newspaper salesman as he cries out, "Special edition!"

The newspaperman is joined by others, and soon a crowd has gathered in the street to read about the new crime, while the camera shows the murderer, still filmed from behind, in the midst of writing, underlining his words while whistling the same tune.

> Since the police denied publicity (*Öffentlichkeit*) to my first letter, I will now turn to the *press!* . . . But *I* have not yet reached the *end.*

Each character in *M* could be the wanted suspect, about whom it is said that he "leaves no traces." Even as he speaks to the world through sensationalistic journalism (as Benjamin notes, an invention of the nineteenth century), he melts into the anonymous crowd of big cities: He is the "man of the crowd," "the type and genius of deep crime" that Edgar Allan Poe mentions in one of his *Tales*. It is a tale Benjamin is eager to cite as an important document on the flâneur and his strange "dialectic."

> Dialectic of flânerie: on one side, the man who feels himself viewed by all and sundry as a true suspect and, on the other side, the man who is utterly undiscoverable, the hidden man.[16]

It is in fact while indulging in flânerie that M, like the characters in *A Tune Just Like That*, will meet the young girl who could have been his second victim. We see him while he is strolling through the streets eating fruit, while a police officer takes advantage of his absence to scour his apartment in search of an "old wooden table" and traces of the "red crayon" that had been used to write the letter to the press. M stops in front of the shop windows, and it is there among the merchandise displayed that he catches the reflection in a mirror of a little girl who grabs his attention. Profoundly troubled, he starts to follow her while whistling his tune. The little girl also stops in front of the display, where she lingers nonchalantly until the moment she sees her mother, the person she was supposed to meet. Disappointed, M continues to whistle in front of a window where a kaleidoscopic image is turning in a spiraling circle. He goes to sit down at a terrace café and swallows down two cognacs one after the other, visibly prey to the obsession signaled by the hit that haunts him. He first attempts to hide his eyes with his clenched fists, as if in order not to see what he sees; then he covers up his ears. Then he leaves, whistling still.

Signaled from offscreen by the hit that he takes along with him wherever he strolls but without appearing on screen, M passes by, not far from the poor blind vendor from whom he had bought the balloon as a gift for his first victim. This vendor, a beggar, recognizes the obsessive melody that trails behind the perambulations of this obsessed murderer like a wake. As surprised as the protagonists of "A Tune Just Like That," he ransacks his memory and ends up figuring out where and when he had heard someone whistling just like that. He then makes the decision to laboriously follow M, groping with his cane, before handing the quest off to another beggar who is younger and, above all, who can see. The clue, which started off as an audible one, passes bit by bit into the visible realm.

In the meantime, M has found himself a new victim, to whom he is giving a piece of fruit: A beautiful orange, it, too, is round, filmed in close-up while he peels it with his knife for the little girl who waits for it on the sidewalk, full of gratitude. This is the moment the young beggar, who has become a detective, chooses to bump up against M in order to mark him with chalk, writing on his back the initial that will allow him to be identified.

M as in murderer (*Mörder*), of course, but also as in music. M, as in a haunting melody, and an obsessive motif, but also as in market or merchandise, whether sonorous, like the hit that haunts him, or visible, like the wares in the store windows where their image is almost melted into the image of his future victim.

M, then: Once this mark is inscribed on M's coat, the police investigation also makes progress. Commissioner Lohmann (Otto Wernicke) has found another clue: The search in M's apartment has revealed the brand of cigarettes he smokes ("Aristons"), which is the same as that of the butts found on the scene of an earlier crime. Returning to M's apartment (while M continues to stroll about with his prey), Lohmann and his assistant also discover the marks left by the murderer's pencil on the windowsill where he wrote his letter to the press. These are the negative traces of what the newspapers had published in black and white: After going from the audible to the visible, the mark seems to become writing and text. The whistled hit, that tune just like that, is inscribed and open to being read and figured out. The cops have their lead, their *tuyau*: "We're finally onto him," Lohmann sighs (*also endlich sind wir auf seiner Spur.*)

Spur, a trace, yes indeed.

Which is to say also the remains, or the rejects, which beggars more than others so often have so much to do with. These very same ragpickers were the object of lively exchanges between Benjamin and Adorno,[17] and it is these recyclers of used commodities who, even before the police, are first onto M, who find his signature mark in the form of an old used-up hit that haunts him and that must be converted into a legible sign, into a clue.

Benjamin's striking remark will have never been as pertinent.

> Neurosis [certainly an understated way of describing M's criminal obsessions] creates the mass-produced article in the psychic economy. There it takes the form of the obsessional idea, which, manufactured in countless copies, appears in the household of the neurotic mind as the ever selfsame.[18]

In short, in the fascinating circulation of circular forms that Fritz Lang sets into motion in between the visible, the audible, and the legible—the balls, the plates, the rounds and refrains, the zeros, the spirals, the pieces of fruit—the hit, the cyclical and obsessive refrain, sings the soul and the psyche of the one who wears, whether right side up (M) or upside down (W), the capital initial of Merchandise (*Ware* in German).

Shadow of a Doubt: Some Songs by Hitchcock

M for music: This is also the very first image that appears after the credits in the *Thirty-Nine Steps* by Hitchcock (1935). M, the initial of "Music Hall," the first of the nine letters that spell out these two words, the first of those capital letters that slide by horizontally, from right to left, across the screen, lighting up one after the other. As is only appropriate, a cymbal crash crowns the appearance of the H for Hitchcock.

Richard Hanny (Robert Donat) has entered into a music hall in London. The show contains "one of the most remarkable men in the world": an artist of memory, a kind of human machine who retains data, a mnemographer of facts and anecdotes whose abilities are always equal to the task. The emcee who introduces him to the audience actually invites the audience to put him to the test ("Test him, please!") before revealing his name: "Mr. Memory."

M as in memory, then, but also as in murder, yet again, for after a brawl turns the show into a riot, Richard finds himself in the street with an unknown woman standing beside him. She asks him for his hospitality, seeking refuge at his place where she will nonetheless be assassinated. Suspected of being guilty of the crime, Richard carries out the investigation. And one of the clues that will put him onto the network of spies responsible for the murder is the return of the melody that was played as Mr. Memory walked on stage. Taken in a car to be interrogated by spies pretending to be police officers, Richard begins to suspect that he is not being driven to a precinct. And, as if by chance, *just like that,* he begins whistling the tune in question. But it is only at the very end of the film that, returning to the very same music hall, he clearly recognizes the melody that announces Mr. Memory's return to the stage. Richard understands that the mnemographer is being used by secret agents to transmit complex and detailed information.

It is at this point that Richard asks Mr. Memory the fatal question: "What are the thirty-nine steps?" And the human memory machine cannot *not* answer: "The thirty-nine steps," he mechanically recites, "is an organization of spies collecting information on behalf of the foreign office of . . ." Yet before being able to pronounce the name of the country, Mr. Memory takes a shot fired by one of the secret agents present in the room.

Amid the general panic, the mnemographer is carried backstage where he lies dying in front of Richard. Richard asks him: "Mr. Memory, what was the secret formula you were taking out of the country?" The dying man hesitates ("Would it be all right telling you?"), but he does not want to "throw away" what was his "biggest job": He recites the entirety of the formula for a complex mechanism—a perfectly silent motor. And before giving up the ghost, he sighs to Richard: "Thank you, thank you. I'm glad it's off my mind. At last."

Two types of memory are at battle here. One is a form of memory that is dead and has become a commodity, one whose mechanical functioning can be admired by anyone who pays their ticket for the music hall. The other is an alive yet buried form of memory that works in hiding. But it is precisely the jingle, if one may say so, for the marvelous mechanical product; it's what indicates Mr. Memory's entry onto the stage, the music with which he advertises his act that makes way for anamnesis in Richard. The little melody, obsessive yet intermittent, marches resolutely toward the final resolution of the enigma that it will have gathered together and condensed within itself from the very beginning. Its reemergence in Richard's consciousness, its breaking to the surface seems, *in fine*, also to liberate the memory merchant grown moribund from his cumbersome merchandise, from his stock of reified data: "It's off my mind, at last," he says just before passing away, before dying as a way of finally becoming alive. That is to say: forgetful.

Three years later, in 1938, with *The Lady Vanishes*, Hitchcock will yet again cast a little melody in the role of spy story hero.[19]

Mrs. Froy (May Whitty), a charming elderly lady who secretly works for England, disappears in a train. Iris (Margaret Lockwood), her young friend, goes off to find her with the help of Gilbert (Michael Redgrave), an ethnomusicologist who is traveling to write his work on the ancient repertoire of popular music and dance. Yet among the other travelers, all possible witnesses declare that they never saw Mrs. Froy. Iris even finds herself being told by a strange doctor that Mrs. Froy never existed, that she was only a hallucination, and that her real name is probably "some past association, an advertisement or a character from a novel, subconsciously remembered."

And yet, there are those letters that Mrs. Froy had written with her finger on the window of the dining car while she was taking tea with Iris: She had inscribed her name as a way of spelling it out to the young woman, and this digital writing stayed there on the windowpane, waiting for a second glance and for the right lighting in order to reemerge, only to disappear once again. In a manner similar to the mnemonic trace in the apparatus of the "magic notepad" that Freud uses as an analogy for the unconscious,[20] the name reappears for an instant before it is erased once again, at the moment when the train, like a train of thought or a train of ideas, enters into the darkness of the tunnel.

Iris and Gilbert end up finding Mrs. Froy. And, since she is a spy, she gives Gilbert a kind of verbal copy of the secret she is transporting to the Foreign Office in London: It's "a tune" that "contains in code, of course, the vital clause of a secret pact between two European countries." Gilbert has to "memorize" it so that the message has "two chances instead of one" of getting to its destination.

In the train taking him to London, Gilbert whistles the melody obsessively; he doesn't let go of it for fear of losing it. And once he arrives with Iris at the Foreign Office, this is exactly what happens. "It's gone," he exclaims. He tries to hum it, but, as Iris herself notes, it's a "wedding march" that comes to mind instead of the message encoded in music. A hymn to marriage, encouraged by Gilbert's nascent love for Iris, that, unconsciously, *just like that*, seems to have substituted itself for the encoded tune. Gilbert can't find the mnemonic trace he's looking for; access to it is barred by his desire for Iris, which is itself represented by another parasite song. Gilbert has become a battlefield for competing musical commodities: "I have forgotten it completely," he ends up confessing.

It is just then that the young couple hears, coming from inside the office outside of whose door they are waiting, the sought-after melody resounding from a piano. The office doors open wide, like doors to a temple into which Iris and

Gilbert seem to have entered to be united *in music.* Mrs. Froy is seated at the piano playing it, and the underground tune, after having been replaced for a moment by the mask of a wedding march, now sounds out like a hymn to the marriage of the reunited lovers.[21]

Unlike *The Thirty-Nine Steps,* where we follow a musical commodity charged with living memory as it slowly rises to the surface, the last scene of *A Lady Vanishes* stages the scene of exchange as one commodity is substituted for another and replaces it. In short, what this finale allows us to see is, to put it in Benjaminian terms, *the marketplace of mass melodic articles in the psychic economy.*

Already in the opening credits of the 1942 film *Shadow of a Doubt,* Hitchcock has a waltz played from an operetta by Franz Lehàr. The waltz is an excerpt from *The Merry Widow,* and it accompanies images of spinning couples. These are images which, in the fade-out that brings us to the first scene, float in a strange way, as if from another era, against the industrial and urban landscape of modern America, before they disappear. The waltz's music also disappears little by little when a close-up shows the face of Charlie (Joseph Cotten), who is lying down on his bed alongside a flurry of scattered bank notes.

When Charlie arrives at his sister's house in the little city of Santa Rosa, we discover both his privileged relationship with his niece, who is also named Charlie, and the suspicions that emerge in her little by little concerning the unexplained resurgence of the waltz that was played during the credits. It's a fairly slow process: The niece, who seems to feel a boundless love for her uncle, tells him she "knows" him, that she knows he doesn't "tell people a lot of things," that "inside you somewhere there is something nobody knows about," something "secret and wonderful." When she adds that she will "find it out," he answers, "It's not good to find out too much, Charlie."

The uncle has a present for his niece: an emerald ring. The gift seems to seal a pact between the two of them, a pact whose terms remain unclear even to them. Mysterious, like the initials engraved on the ring. He has just placed it onto her finger when the waltz from the credits sounds out again, yet again accompanying the same dreamlike images of spinning couples. While serving coffee, the young Charlie sings it insistently, so much so that her younger sister, as serious as an adult, pronounces, in a disapproving tone, a phrase that sounds proverbial: "Sing at the table and you'll marry a crazy husband." As if the ring, in a way that remains hidden to all, had sealed a disastrous parody of marriage.

Over the course of the rest of the dinner, the niece, who is still humming along, starts up a fascinating and remarkable conversation, just like that, about obsessive melodies, about tunes *just like that*. Here is the conversation, whose screenplay or dialogue could have been written by Theodor Reik, the author of *The Haunting Melody*:

THE NIECE: I can't get that tune out of my head; maybe if somebody tells me what it is, I'll forget it.

THE MOTHER: It's a waltz.

THE NIECE: I know it is, but which one? You know [she goes on while the camera shows Uncle Charlie's strangely preoccupied face] it's the funniest thing, sometimes I get a tune in my head like that and, suddenly, I hear somebody else humming it, too. I think tunes jump from head to head. Do you know what it is, Uncle Charlie?

THE UNCLE: Um, no, no, I, I don't know what it is.

THE MOTHER: I remember, um, it's on the tip of my tongue. It's a waltz and it's Victor Herbert.

THE LITTLE BROTHER: Victor Herbert wasn't a waltz.

This scene is almost a strange form of musical telepathy: The melody, as if it were *just like that*, as if it had a soul and an autonomous will, not only insists, but seems to want to pass from mouth to mouth and from memory to memory. Yet at the very moment it seems to be making its way through its anamnesis in minds haunted by it, and against the resistance they put up, a cascade of metonymic displacements prevents it from being identified, or at least delays its identification, deferring its becoming-conscious and being named. Victor Herbert, who was a cellist in Johann Strauss's orchestra in Vienna before emigrating to the United States, where he composed many operettas until his death in 1924, is indeed not a waltz, as the little brother with his trivial childhood wisdom puts it, underlining the metonym of the author for the work. Yet the author in question, though metonymically linked to the waltz through the implicit name of Johann Strauss, hides the veritable patronymic, Franz Lehàr, and the incriminating title, the clue that will lead back to the crimes of Uncle Charlie, someone who is sought after as the assassin of several "merry widows" whom he has robbed of their money and jewels: that ring that he just gave to his niece, for example.

The uncle is more and more disturbed by this and he, in turn, offers a false title.

THE UNCLE: It's the Blue Danube waltz.

THE NIECE: Oh, yes, of course it is. No it isn't, Uncle Charlie, that's not what it is, I know what it is, it's the *Merry* . . .

Here, at the first word of the title, Uncle Charlie is trapped and has no other way out of the situation but to knock over a glass, interrupting the conversation that was getting ready to turn out badly for him. We still do not know the full title of the tune.

Several days later, the niece, whose suspicions about her uncle have grown, is trying to piece back together a page of the newspaper that her uncle had ripped up. Faced with the impossibility of putting all of the pieces of the puzzle back together, she decides to go to the municipal library to read the news she is looking for, with a mixture of hope (will she be able to dissipate the doubts weighing on her about her beloved uncle?) and fear. She arrives just in time; the library is in the process of closing. She finds the issue of the newspaper and mumbles as she flips through it: "It can't be anything really awful." But she is given pause when she sees the title of the article: "Where is the Merry Widow Murderer? Nation-wide Search Under Way for Strangler of Three Rich Women." In the name of one of the three victims, she also recognizes the initials engraved on her emerald ring. Shocked, she stands up and walks through the library like a sleepwalker as the fateful waltz is heard, once again accompanied by the images of the spinning dancers who remain superimposed onto the next shot, where we see the uncle, the next morning, reading his newspaper while walking in the garden.

Young Charlie, who has slept almost all day, doesn't come out of her room until evening to help her mother prepare dinner. In the kitchen, her mother is humming the waltz distractedly. Charlie tells her:

> Now you're humming that waltz. Whatever you do, please don't hum that tune any more. I just got it out of

> my head and I don't want to get it started again. Please remember don't hum that tune!

After having served as a clue over the course of its slow and insistent rise to consciousness, the waltz has become undesirable. Like an unwelcome guest, like that criminal uncle for whom it is the metonym.

"Tunes jump from head to head." With this line from Charlie, Hitchcock seems to give the formula for the fetishism of musical merchandise when it's taken to an extreme. As if tunes were animated, *as if they were just like that*, endowed with a soul and with the autonomous capacity for movement that makes them circulate in the collective psyche. For in this case, the circulation of the hit is no longer part of the restricted economy of individual memory: At the table that unites an extended family, it becomes a *telepathic* vehicle, the motif or the motor, the motive for affecting things from a distance, for cascades of anamneses and for chains of repressed material.

From *The Thirty-Nine Steps* to *Shadow of a Doubt* by way of *A Lady Vanishes*, Hitchcock compiles a veritable criminological and economic treatise on musical obsession for the screen: He stages not only the hit's function as an anamnestic agent but also its exchanges and its substitutions, its twisted metonymies and circulation.

CHAPTER 4 Capital's Intimate Hymn

Forbidden Melody

On the 1978 album *Ex-Fan des Sixties,* Jane Birkin sang a great song by Serge Gainsbourg. It was called "Mélodie interdite" ("Forbidden Melody"):

> It is forbidden to pass/Through this melody/It is forbidden to go/Through that tune/This melody is private/Strictly forbidden danger . . ./What this melody recalls to me/Is strictly confidential.[1]

What did Birkin and Gainsbourg want to tell us, or not to tell us? What song were they singing for us by speaking of a forbidden melody?

Of course, hearing their words ("what this melody recalls to me/Is strictly confidential"), we are ready, all too ready even, to understand what they mean: The tune they are singing, the tune they forbid us to go through, suggests illicit thoughts; it represents what is better kept quiet and secret. Like Reik's haunting melodies that come back from the unconscious, like M the criminal's whistling, or like "a tune just like that" passed at the table between Charlie and

Charlie. It is a melody, then, meant to be hidden and censored but having inopportunely escaped this censorship.

And yet this forbidden melody—*this very one* that itself sings and says that it must remain confidential—this melody that points to itself in the song does not seem to enunciate or reveal anything that deserves to be censored. In the end, it is nothing but a pure promise or instance of something forbidden without any determinable content. A little bit like "I Came to Tell You That I'm Leaving" ("*Je suis venu te dire que je m'en vais*") seemed to be a pure structure of confession deferring itself, always waiting to be fulfilled.

As it happens, this "Forbidden Melody," like other exemplary songs we have listened to, seems to want to state a certain logic or economy of obsessive melodies that hits, in the sense we have given them here, are. It is by listening to hits themselves that we have been led to question their fetishistic phantasmagorias, their self-desiring scenes, their quest for the unique through repetition, their comings and goings, and their particular way of articulating the psyche with the market. This "Forbidden Melody" also invites us to question something that appears to be one of the motors of the strange life of hits: censorship. For if, as our brief cinematic study of earworms has shown us, hits are related to the drive to confess, it's because they are fed by a very close complicity between obsession and prohibition: It may well be that hits are always, potentially, forbidden melodies on the verge of being censored. And this characteristic is perhaps even what gives them their singular capacity to *reiterrupt*: It makes of them, and we will get back to this, a kind of unmentionable hymn.

But we do not yet know what a forbidden *melody* is exactly. Nor what *musical* censorship would be, if it exists at all.

And this is why we must first briefly turn to the history of censorship in music, because it can help enlighten us about the confessional structure of hits. This history has yet to be written, and it should be considered in the context, once again, of the Benjaminian analogy between the market and the psyche: that is, as the history of a form of censorship that, on the global political and economic stage where hits are produced, reproduces on a much larger scale the mechanisms of repression at work in the unconscious.[2]

To take a recent example, one need only remember that, in the United States, in the months following the September 11, 2001, attacks, censorship concentrated on a certain number of hit songs that, apparently, or rather in too audible a way, transmitted thoughts that had become unmentionable in that context. This was, in a way, an exercise in collective repression within the circulation of musical commodities formed by hits. This campaign for denial reached its height when the Texan company Channel Communications (owner of more than a thousand radio stations in the United States) published a list of songs to be banned that included some five hundred titles.[3]

It so happens that in each case, it was only a question of the lyrics to the songs: Either they referred to aviation (as was the case with Elton John's "Bennie and the Jets") or they transmitted a message perceived as indecently pacifistic, like John Lennon's "Imagine" or Louis Armstrong's "What a Wonderful World," both of which were censored.

In a way, even the censorship of music *in general*, under the Taliban regime in Afghanistan, for example, seems to have as its object *what music represents* other than itself, that is to say, what it refers to: as if, in this particular case, it transmitted a general text, the "libretto" of Western capitalist culture.[4]

It is not of course a question of minimizing the sinister consequences of what are, in effect, clear cases of censorship, but of wondering *what*, in each case, is effectively being censored. In these cases, what is being censored is, for the vast majority, either *music in general*, or else one or another of the *messages* that a given piece of music is said to transmit through its words or images. In short, it seems to me that it is very rare that any *particular* melody has ever been censored *for itself*.[5] This is so much the case that I cannot think of any instance of a forbidden *melody*, excluded from the circulation of commodities on the economic market. No more than there would seem to be any melody forbidden on the psychic market, as Reik's inquiry into obsessive melodies attested, in spite of itself and along with its failure: What a melody hides—and the reason why it may therefore have to remain hidden—is always, in the last (psycho)analysis, words or images.

An official censor of theaters in Victorian England—the Examiner of Plays—who was charged in particular with the task of examining Verdi's operas, went so far as to declare: "My business is not with the music of an opera, but with the libretto."[6] If we take the word "libretto" in its extended sense, including in it everything that could be called "the extramusical," this Victorian censor would be mostly correct.

One may object that a given genre of music—rock and roll, for example, or jazz—has been censored as such. But leaving aside the fact that it is therefore a question of genre and not of melody, we might also ask in this case: What exactly is a genre of music *as such*?

It so happens that a history of musical censorship (which remains to be written) would no doubt be the most effective deconstruction of an idea that came from the first wave of

German romanticism: the idea of *absolute music.*[7] Even a style of music as controversial as jazz was in Europe in the 1930s and '40s, and which is for the most part wordless, was able to get around censorship through its words: As a historian[8] has bemusedly pointed out, Louis Armstrong's music was able to get through the ideological customs office of fascist repression without changing one single note. Armstrong's *name* was translated into Italian as Luigi Bracciaforte. If this Italian "Louis Strongarm" was able to provide a passport for Louis Armstrong's trumpet and voice, it is certainly the sign of the fact that censorship did not bear on the music itself, but on proper names, which were in their turn suspected of smuggling in common names—"black," for example.

If, as these brief historical considerations suggest, it is indeed the case that censorship has never targeted a melody as such, what in the world is a song like "Forbidden Melody" trying to say to us? What is it talking about?

As we have seen, it does not pronounce anything that has to be hidden, kept out of sight, or held secret. It basically does nothing else but give voice to the pure movement of a becoming-secret without any determinate content; it does nothing but sing the song's retreat and retraction, which is the precise counterpoint to its capacity to reemerge: "I'm going away," it says; I'm hiding or retracting into myself, because it is from this retreat that I have been able to "come to tell you that . . ."

A similar movement animates Aretha Franklin's 1970 hit "Don't Play That Song (You Lied)." In that song, she sings:

> Don't play that song for me/'Cause it brings back memories/Of days that I once knew,/The days I spent

> with you./Oh no, don't let him play it,/It fills my heart with pain . . ./I remember just what he said./He said darling, "Darling, I love you,"/And I know that he lied,/ "Darling, I love you,"/You know that you lied.[9]

It does of course seem to be the case that the "you" interpellated here is the guy being confronted by the cheated or abandoned girl in a restaging of the eternal love story that hits are. But it is also just as often the song itself: "that song" we are all hearing and that sings itself in the paradoxical form of a prohibition of itself. It prohibits itself—"Don't play"—the better to capitalize, in a way, on its power to emerge when it will come back to tell us that . . . It censors itself the better to lock itself up, to seal up its secret without a secret, to define or encrypt the form of an intimacy without content, open to any appropriation. And, in doing so, it also and perhaps above all states the affective potential—or better yet, the potential affect—contained in the hit.

It is indeed the case that censoring a hit or prohibiting it, refusing its right to exist and to be reproduced in souls and on the market of minds, is basically the same thing as recognizing its incomparable power over the psyche as a ghost. For the song, insofar as it comes and comes back to tell us that . . . , insofar as it does not stop bringing itself to the point of saying or of confessing but without saying or confessing anything at all, has an unheard-of strength in what we have named its reiterruptions. It has the power hymns have to rally us and carry us away: as the earworm that haunts us, it is an intimate hymn, a kind of "Marseillaise" of the psyche—irrepressible, compulsive, and impossible to stop.

* * *

It is therefore almost certainly not just by chance that certain hits become hymns, official ones. This is notably the case with "Imagine," the overplayed song by John Lennon that was censored, as we have seen, for its pacifistic message in the wake of 9/11.

The song was a "gift," writes Irene Khan, the general secretary of Amnesty International, when Yoko Ono, Lennon's widow, authorized the humanitarian organization to use the song for a campaign launched in 2003. She continues:

> "Imagine" expresses the hope and idealism that inspire Amnesty International's vision: that of a world in which every person enjoys all of the rights enshrined in the Universal Declaration of Human Rights. In its appeal to the power of imagination, the song echoes Amnesty International's faith in the power of the ordinary individual to make a difference.[10]

As the song for the unity and reconciliation of the world, from "me" to "us" ("I hope some day you will join us/And the world will live as one"), "Imagine" has begun to share the fate reserved for the "Hymn to Joy," from the finale to Beethoven's Ninth Symphony, which was chosen in 1972 by the Council of Europe as its official hymn. Without its German words, of course, without Schiller's poem and its famous line (*Alle Menschen werden Brüder*, "All men will become brothers"), but keeping this ideal as a subtext in the purportedly supranational language of music.

Without claiming to incarnate such universal values, "Georgia on My Mind," a big hit for Ray Charles in 1960,[11] is another example of this becoming-hymn. In effect, the song now figures in the code of the state of Georgia. It was officially inscribed into the state's legal registers on April 24,

1979, and one can read, in chapter 50–3 of the aforementioned code, in section 60: "The song 'Georgia on My Mind' . . . is designated as the official song of the state of Georgia." The words follow:

> Georgia, Georgia, the whole day through/Just an old sweet song keeps Georgia on my mind . . .

Like so many other songs, "Georgia" sings its own capacity to remember, as if it had always been destined to play this role of a memorial sign, of a (self-)commemorating monument. But the becoming-hymn of "Georgia" is also a sign of political reconciliation: Ray Charles had canceled a planned 1961 concert in Augusta to protest against the racist "Jim Crow"[12] laws that were in effect until 1965.

Yet beyond these particular instances and a few others, what is at stake here is a kind of general hymnology that is not limited to hymns that have been officially recognized as such. For the becoming-hymn of hits is elaborated not only on national and international political stages but also on the stage of the individual psyche, with all the obsessive melodies Reik analyzes or that film so often stages: musical obsessions that, in each one of us, play the role of an "Internationale" of intimate commemorations.

There is here, in sum, a kind of *inthymnacy*, an anthemic intimacy that blurs the borders between the private and the public. It produces, as Proust put it, "the national anthem of [our] love,"[13] or of our desire.

To confess, to be confessed, or to be censored as soon as it becomes translatable.

Money: Music, Money, and Wit

But are we really so sure that what hits sing about is our desire, our shameful love, or anything else that we would prefer to keep to ourselves, buried deep in the well-guarded heart of an absolutely unique self? When they interrupt us like a Freudian slip or an *acte manqué*, when, as they do in *Same Old Song*, they come to (make us) say something we'd rather keep quiet, are we really so sure that they are speaking about what is most properly ours?

As we have repeatedly emphasized, these intimate hymns that seem to serve the purpose of tying the subject to itself in its uniqueness and singularity, these *inthymns* are also at the same time clichés: what is most banal on the market of musical commodities, what is most interchangeable in the circulation of exchange. In short, these hits are so much like ourselves and so clearly bring us together because they all look exactly alike.

In sum, hits are the anthemic vehicles for a singular and clandestine intimacy, even as they are also perfectly common musical commodities absolutely equivalent and indifferent to one another. Faced with this paradox of hits that insists and resists each time we think we have figured it out, what we must once again attempt to understand is a certain homology between the market and the psyche, for this is the paradox that feeds the production of hits, one that hits themselves perhaps help produce and construct.

In order to better understand this homology, we need to take one last detour: after Marx, Benjamin, and Kierkegaard, after Resnais, Fritz Lang, and Hitchcock, Freud and Kant will bring us to what may well be the final enigma of these hits that haunt us: the intimate anthem that they belt out in the depths of our self about the glory of exchange. As if they incited or edified within us, each time in a singular way, the inthymnity of capital and of general equivalence.

* * *

In his *Psychoanalysis of Song* [*Psychanalyse de la chanson*], Philippe Grimbert compares the "creation of songs" to the phenomenon of the joke (*Witz* in German), to which Freud paid considerable attention.[14] When Charles Trenet confides, "I am not the one who chooses my songs; they choose me," or when Julien Clerc says, "All of a sudden one is visited and finds this thing that comes from who knows where," or when Francis Lemarque explains how "the song . . . breaks into me like a robber, curls up in a corner of my memory, and then I forget about it, and a little while later it reappears in a kind of enchantment"—all these testimonies concord, in the perspective of the psychoanalyst, to indicate an "unconscious emergence," which is the same one that can be observed in the *Witz*, the Freudian slip, or the *acte manqué*.

Freud has shown how *Witz* works through irruptive and symptomatic manifestations, in its apparent spontaneity as a joke. For Freud, these instances actually participate in a complex psychic economy made up of substitutions, exchanges, and transactions between the sayable and the unsayable. This is in fact why, as a way of enlightening us about the genesis of a joke, Freud suggests an analogy that has now become quite familiar to us: "We can allow ourselves to compare the psychic economy to a commercial enterprise," with its expenses, investments, and profits.

We have already encountered the structural homology between the psyche and the market in Benjamin's very striking remark that neurosis produces "the mass-produced article in the psychic economy" in the form of the "obsessive idea." And we need to spend some more time with this idea, so much is it the case that hits, in several ways and on several different levels, are also, like jokes, certainly *economic* phenomena. For if the hit itself is a question of value, money, currency, and exchange, this is not only because it is a mass musical commodity generating considerable profits but also because it is an earworm, an obsessive melody that continues to reproduce itself in innumerable copies in the souls of the melomaniacs that we are.

It is surprising that Freud, who takes care to remind us extensively of what philosophers and writers have had to say about *Witz*, mentions Kant only in passing (when he refers to "the comedic in general"). He could have found, however, in the very paragraph of the *Critique of Judgment* to which he briefly alludes (§54), a detailed analysis of several jokes, which in several particular ways announces an *economic* conception of the phenomenon.

But if Kant will retain our interest here, it is not because he is a possible unrecognized precursor to the Freudian theory of jokes. It is rather because he is no doubt the first to have begun to see that successful songs, which he would in fact have hated, are closely related to jokes and the economy of exchanges that produce them.

It is indeed the case that Kant saw little value in music, especially in pure music without words and without a message, all music that does not transmit an idea. In his *Critique of Judgment*, he declared, as if speaking of our tunes *just like that*, of the melodies and little ditties whose words say nothing, or very little:

> Where fine arts are not, either closely or remotely, brought into combination with moral ideas . . . they then only serve for a diversion, of which one continually feels an increasing need in proportion as one has availed oneself of it as a means of dispelling one's discontented mind, with the result that one makes oneself ever more

and more unprofitable and dissatisfied with oneself. (§52, "The combination of the fine arts in one and the same product")[15]

If for Kant music is therefore a pure distraction when it has nothing serious or moral to say, it is understandable when, in the next paragraph (§53), he declares it provides "nothing lasting." It is "an agreeable rather than a fine art" (160), and, if it can incite or allow "ideas" to emerge, it is only in a playful way, as if by chance, along the path of sonorous sensations: "the play of thought *incidentally* excited by it being merely the effect of a more or less mechanical association" (156, emphasis added). A kind of *free* association, one is tempted to say (in an admittedly non-Kantian way), which is not related to reflection or to ideas. This is why, ranking it at the bottom of the fine arts, Kant compares music to jokes and puns: Music and jokes, he writes, "afford gratification . . . by mere force of change."[16]

What "change" is he talking about?

Wechsel, says Kant in German. In other words, and perhaps more precisely, *exchange*. (It is indeed the case that in Germany, places where one can exchange one monetary currency for another have the label *Geldwechsel* written above them.)

But what kind of exchange is then at work in music and in jokes?

For Kant, what is at stake in the one and in the other is a kind of play in which "aesthetic ideas, or even representations of the understanding," alternate, are exchanged with one another, "by which, all said and done, nothing is thought." And if, once we accept that this is the case, they only follow one another as a pure, alternating exchange (*Wechsel*), if that is the nature of the "lively gratification" that they give us, one must certainly conclude that, from this perpetual exchange, nothing remains: It "leaves nothing behind."

In short, for Kant, music—and especially the kind of music we would today call light music, pop songs that do not transmit "moral ideas" with the words they sing—would share with *Witz* a symbolic economy that produces nothing, contenting itself with the pleasure of exchange and only for the pleasure of exchange. A psychoanalyst of song was able to tell us that a hit and a joke are comparable in their genesis or their inspiration, but Kant indicates that they are even more profoundly related to one another to the extent that, in the end, they have nothing to say beyond the naked exposition of this structure of interchangeability, general equivalence, and circulation.

In the end, they would do nothing more than *lend themselves to*. Lend themselves to *exchange*.

The shallowness of an exchange without any remainder or anchor is also that of money. In the *Doctrine of Right* section of *The Metaphysics of Morals*, Kant describes money in the following way:

> *Money* is a thing that can only be *used* by being *alienated*. . . . [I]t *represents* all goods . . . having no value in itself. . . . The value of money is only indirect. One cannot enjoy money itself or make immediate use of it in any way.[17]

In sum, money has only an exchange value. It has no use value (it is, to use Marx's terms, the "general equivalent").

Yet the shallowness of money is what many hits sing about and expose. They do so by playing on the ambivalence between what they seem to denounce as the absence of any proper value to money and their own interchangeability, as hits that will always be improper and equivalent to one another in exchange.

One need only remember "Money," for an example, sung by Michael Jackson on the 1995 album *HIStory* (reported to have sold eighteen million copies). As the album's title suggests, the songs that appear on it speak of the singer himself (it's *his story*, the story of his success). Also, and no doubt in an involuntary way, the refrain presents the kind of auto-referential irony with which we are now familiar: *Anything, anything, anything for money*, hammers the refrain; who cares, the hit itself seem to sing, who cares what I sing, it will always be as good as the equivalent of something else, even if it will never be worth something in and of itself.

Yet it is Pink Floyd, with their famous 1973 hit "Money" (from the album *Dark Side of the Moon*, a massive commercial success reported to have sold over thirty-five million copies), who delivers the formula of equivalence between the two forms of general equivalence represented by money and by hits: *Money*, they begin by singing, *it's a gas*, a gas that evaporates without remainder into its exchanges, without leaving anything of its own behind. Then, in the next verse, *Money! It's a hit!* Pink Floyd literally states the case that money is a hit. Between money and the hit, between the one and the other, each of them worth something for the other even as they are worth both nothing and everything, and that's all there is: the equivalence of values.[18]

Many other successful songs sing about money, that general equivalent: "Money Money Money" by the group Abba, or Billy Joel's "Easy Money." Yet the number one place in this musico-numismatic Top 50 no doubt goes to "Money

Honey," interpreted by the Drifters in 1953, and then covered in 1956 by Elvis Presley.

"Money Honey" is in effect general circulation set to song: the circulation of money and of people, of men and women, exchanging the one for the other, duping each other, and taking the place of one another indefinitely.

In the first verse, a landlord rings the doorbell. And when the lyrical "I" asks, "What's on your mind?" he answers: "Money, honey" (repeated three times), "if you want to get along with me."

There is a change of scene in the second verse: the lyrical "I" calls to "the woman that I loved best." She in turn asks him, "What you want with me?" and the lyrical "I" answers her, over and over again, "Money, honey" (three times), "if you want to get along with me."

Third sequence, third verse: the lyrical "I" gets angry and asks "baby" to tell him "face to face/how could another man take my place." And, faced with this question that, by exchanging protagonists, widens monetary exchange to the interchangeability of people and pronouns, she answers yet again: "Money, honey (three times), if you want to get along with me."

The moral of this hit-fable in the ear of advanced capitalism is in effect the generalization of general equivalence, since, as the lyrical "I" puts it, "the women may come and the women may go/but before I say I love you so/I want money, honey [three times], if you want to get along with me . . ."

Fame

Putting all jokes—and *Witz* and puns—aside, let us return to Kant to try to get back to ourselves, if that is possible. To ourselves, to what we are or think we properly are, before or after our places and roles have been exchanged, like somewhat used parts circulating to the rhythm of hits.

I don't know what Kant would have thought of Brassens's 1952 song "La Mauvaise reputation." Whatever he may have thought, for the austere thinker of Königsberg, one must always take seriously and avoid playing with what belongs properly to the deceased: surviving memory, reputation, and renown, in short with the *bona fama defuncti*, as he puts it in his *Doctrine of Right*, several pages after his paragraph on money. This paragraph is itself followed by another on books and their counterfeit, and then, after considerations on inheritance, by a conclusion devoted to "good reputation after one's death."

Why this strange sequence from money to books and inheritance, to conclude with the *fama defuncti*? It is because it is still a question of possession, of what is proper and what is property when Kant speaks of acquiring a "good reputation" (*einen guten Namen erwerben*). This renown, he says, that will remain even though the *homo phaenomenon* will no longer exist; this *fama* of the deceased is the deceased's own good (*das Seine*), what belongs to him or her, what is his or her own. But it is a good that surprises Kant, even as he recognizes it is incontestable in law: "It would be absurd to think that someone who has died can still possess something after his death (and so when he no longer exists), as if what he left behind were a thing (*Sache*)."[19]

This *fama* we may someday have—without ever being able to possess it, since we will no longer be here to do so and since it is no more a *thing* than is money—this renown in which our name will perhaps still survive is therefore a very particular kind of possession. Though it is ours, we will no longer be able to have and detain it, though it is probably even more properly ours than all of our other properties, since it resumes or crystallizes afterward what will have been, what will no longer change or be exchanged, what is no longer open to becoming anything else. This possession that is not one is life, which, *post mortem*, has taken form: which has become *a* life.

Hits, we were saying, not only willfully sing about money, but they also, in their own way, sing the fact that they have money's structure: that of exchange and general equivalence. Hits are worth nothing in and of themselves; all they do is to be equivalent to something else. They are equivalent among themselves and are always worth something else—worth whatever value we may want to *invest* in them.

And yet, what they seem most predisposed to take on is precisely what has crystallized as a life, or as a slice of life: what has taken form to become something unique, a property like no other. An instant, a summer, a year that has become incomparably ours, but ours only once it is lost, because it is dead and impossible to possess.

Yes, what many hits sing and have us sing about is that *fama* or renown of a perhaps secret and certainly singular moment, which survives in the strange manner of a most proper possession that one no longer possesses. And, yet again, hits sing about this survival by singing about their own renown, in the void of the auto-referential structure that they are and which lends itself all the better to all exchanges because it is worth nothing on its own.

Many a hit seems to want to ensure its own reputation by attempting in some way to climb up the posthumous hit parade of songs that will survive their time. The paradigmatic example of this is probably "Fame," the song interpreted by Irene Cara and covered in the eponymous 1980 film by

Alan Parker. It is difficult, once again, to translate lyrics that are both so banal and remarkable, that have gone around the world and into so many ears without our having really paid attention. The ridicule that attends any attempt to translate the lyrics—and one always feels very awkward in doing so—is probably not without relation to a certain self-censorship of the hit, which speaks and survives all the better in us because its words are so easily forgotten. Translating them, I have the feeling that I am spreading a secret that was a secret to no one, or that I am exchanging the unexchangeable: that singular knot that ties the words of a language to the refrain that carries them. Anyway, at the risk of damaging the *bona fama* of fame through this mechanism of linguistic exchange, here it is:

> Rappelle-toi mon nom—Renommée—Je vivrai pour toujours—J'apprendrai à voler—Là-haut . . . —J'arriverai jusqu'au ciel—J'allumerai le ciel comme une flamme—Renommée—Je vivrai pour toujours—*Baby*, rappelle-toi mon nom—rappelle-toi, rappelle-toi.[20]

Here again, although the hit is trying to affirm itself for forever, it doesn't sing anything at all. It is, in other words, that pure structure of exchange, of *lending itself to*, but more than ever closed in on itself: remember, the lyrical "I" tells us, that I am called fame, that my own title, as a hit, my name, is Fame (*Fama*), that I am therefore only the echoed repetition of myself and my proper name (*name, fame*), now and forever. And remember above all that I am only that, a reminder, a call to remember, to name and rename whatever you want. Everything and nothing: everything, anything, *anything for money or fame*, because nothing, nothing proper in particular.

Although in a less pure way, many other hits also speak of their own fame, and in so doing they themselves offer, with hospitality of unequalled force, a fantasmatic exchange for our own. I am thinking of Claude François singing *Cette année-là* ("That Year") in 1976.

> That year/I was singing for the first time./The audience didn't know me,/What a year that year was . . ./It was just yesterday, but today nothing has changed,/It's the same job that starts again tonight,/It was in 1962. . . .[21]

In 1962 (the year mentioned by the song) just as in 1976 (the year it was released), it's still the same thing; nothing changes. Over and over the hit sings its survival, its *fama*, its success, and it sings it *to itself.* Always the same but each time other, something no one, no "I," no *homo phaenomenon* can possess, but which circulates among everyone, from the one to the other, ad infinitum.

To everyone, to all mortals, the hit, by saying "I," sings that no, it will not be me, I will not disappear that way. *Oh no, not I,* as in Gloria Gaynor's big hit "I Will Survive" (1979). Under the pretext of speaking of a way of surviving the end of a love affair, and before any girl or guy can identify with it, the song also enunciates the survival of the hit itself in the now familiar ambiguity that changes the musical self into the voice of the song itself:

> You think I'd lay down and die,/Oh no, not I/I will survive,/ . . . I know I will stay alive,/I've got all my life to live,/ . . . and I'll survive,/I will survive.

By singing about its own survival, the hit constitutes itself as the structure of auto-commemoration that it is. At bottom, it is nothing other than *fama* itself, renown that renames, survival that survives. And this is why, duping us, it charges itself with the affect of every unique moment as a way of repeating it ad infinitum, of drawing it into the enclosure of a secret that defers its circulation while waiting for its eternal return.

The hit capitalizes on lived time, any lived time, which it subtracts from the market of exchanges (*I am leaving*) only the better to reinvest in it (*I came to tell you that . . . remember . . . I will survive . . .*). And once the singular moment commemorated by the hit comes back in its indifferent fidelity to everything and nothing, it comes back augmented by the nostalgic interest of an "*I was there.*" "I was there!" wrote Fellini in his notes for a music video he never made:

> Time past. Faraway eras . . . I remember them well, I see them. I was there; I have always been there.[22]

And it is yet again Fellini who, in an interview with Lucio Dalla, one of Italy's greatest singers and the author of many a hit, declares:

> I am convinced that if, at the end of our lives, we were allowed to say something, and if we were truly sincere, we would sing a little song as a summary of an entire existence [*riassunto di tutta un'esistenza*]. I realized this with the four or five motifs that always invade me with the same nostalgia, the same emotion, the same regret [*lo stresso rimpianto*]. (Ibid.)

One would be hard-pressed to better state the inherent melancholy of any "sound-track-to-life," insofar as it is only ours when it no longer truly can be. But this melancholy is indissociable from the affect most proper to hits, from the properly improper affect provided by their *overwhelming boredom*, for the little song that summarizes an entire existence and seems to want to contain a slice of life for eternity is also what inscribes the inthymnity of exchange and of general equivalence into the psyche's space and time.

Hits, those capital inventions of advanced capitalism, are constantly converting the unique into the cliché. And vice versa.

CHAPTER 5 *Around the World: Around Oneself*

Hits now go all around the world. They accompany the very movement of globalization and the expansion of the market. From the outside—toward new markets to be conquered—and from the inside—in the commodification of the psyche.

This is what the duo Daft Punk was singing about in 1997 in "Around the World": a hundred and forty times, if I've counted correctly, the pure and simple repetition of this phrase, "around the world," which will have thereby made its way through the world by constantly turning around itself.

How many times have I walked, in the street, in the metro, in some store, to the sound of this hit that dictated my cadence, just like the robots one can see in Michel Gondry's video for the song? I have no idea. But each and every time, there was an unspeakably bittersweet melancholy that made the world look small, as round as a phonogram, narrow and nonetheless infinite, like the place where general interchangeability is constantly exchanged with absolute singularity.

This affect of exchange now has, for us at least, a name and an exemplary figure: the hit, what Boris Vian has called *le tube*. That is to say, the earworm that multiplies through innumerable copies of itself, proliferating musical commodities on the global market but also in us, in each one of us. And it does so without looking like it does: *Just like that*, it becomes an essential hinge, a link between the market and the psyche. By identifying with the banal, nondescript "I" that speaks in hits, by adopting and incorporating the autoproductive and self-desiring structure that they are—they who so willfully stage their own repetition—we allow ourselves to be haunted and inhabited by the merchandise that infinitely reproduces itself in us, in our heart of hearts. We espouse its point of view or of listening, along with the logic of general equivalence that regulates its commercial life. This logic is the logic of money: The indifference or the indifferentiation of hits is infinitely welcoming because it is indefinitely indifferent.

We too, actually, are largely indifferent to these hits that live in us, with us, perhaps even *as* us, but as if in spite of ourselves. Most of the time, we do not understand, and do not want to understand, what they are saying, the story they are telling. We listen to them without lending them an ear, welcoming them grudgingly, thinking we must be deaf to the worn-out words and washed-out lyrics carried by these manufactured melodic products diffused on such a large scale. Yet it is precisely because we do not want to get anything out of musical commodities—upon which we impose a censorship unaware of itself—it is for this very reason that they are all the more ready to reemerge when we are least expecting it, without our having called them up or desired them. They come back then, these haunting melodies; they come back in us and in spite of ourselves to speak to us about us. They even make us gain *access* to ourselves.

This is the paradox that we have attempted to follow as it works its way between Reik's melo-psychoanalytical experiments and Kierkegaard's essay in experimental psychology: *Access to the self*, to what is most singular and hidden within oneself, only comes from what is absolutely ordinary. It only opens up—if it opens up—in the experience of banality and of the cliché.

Or rather, and more precisely, access to the self, when it takes on the form of melodic haunting, when its door is cracked ajar thanks to the sudden appearance of a haunting or obsessive tune that is looking to clear a path through the censorship opposed to it, this *access* is both a passage and, according to another sense of the word, a *crisis*. An access *to* oneself and an outbreak *of* oneself (in French, one speaks of an *accès de fièvre*, or an outbreak of fever). The "I" who is the subject of and subject to these kinds of access—call them melomaniacs or musically obsessed—does indeed go through the ordeal of himself or herself. In a manner analogous to what Kierkegaard calls *repetition*, the listener experiences a blockage, stopped up and stagnant repetition, as if he were his own cliché, a Nuremberg image of himself, whence *perhaps* will suddenly emerge the flight and enthusiasm of the return to what is most singularly proper to oneself: *I was there*, he says to himself then, thanks to the little song that haunts him; I was there; here is what I have lived like no one else, what was and is no longer.

All hits harbor this nostalgia and melancholy, even the most joyful ones, because they make us recry (*rimpiangere*, as Fellini would say) what we can find only in its loss, that to which we gain access only to be immediately banished from it. Banished from the banal which is nonetheless where the chance of the unique resides: Such is this nonetheless overwhelming affect without affect of infinitely repeated general exchange, both in the movements of the commercial world and in the psychic economy.

With any of the songs that make their way around the world and that each seem to have the same value as any other, it sometimes happens that I make my way around myself. That is, I feel like I've already made my way, as the expression goes, around the question I should be for myself: Nothing else is expected but the circular repetition of the cliché that I am (*you are a cliché*, someone tells John Travolta in the beautiful and very sad *Saturday Night Fever*). And yet, it is in the melodic obsession found in this repetition of the whatever that the unique is lodged, if there is any: Somewhere, in a place without place, the reserve of an excess is held, in me but without belonging to me.

In 1973, Roberta Flack had a huge hit with "Killing Me Softly with His Song." I'll leave the last word to her—because she tells me what I am, as if I were not there. This song also made its way around the world. As if it knew all of us in our most intimate details, but also as if we were not there.

> *Singing my life with his words, killing me softly with his song . . . he sang as if he knew me in all my dark despair and then he looked right through me as if I wasn't there.*

CHAPTER 6 *The Blood of the Cut and the Promise of the Breakthrough*

This is the point to which, above all, the attention of our rulers should be directed—that music and gymnastic be preserved in their original form, and no innovation made. They must do their utmost to maintain them intact . . . for any musical innovation is full of danger to the whole State, and ought to be prohibited. When modes of music change, the fundamental laws of the State always change with them.

—Plato, *Republic*, 424b–c

. . . that Tune so cherished by the Swiss that they have forbidden it from being played by their Troops on pain of death, since it would cause those who heard it to dissolve in tears, desert, or die, so much would it arouse in them the ardent desire to see their country again.

—Jean-Jacques Rousseau, *Dictionary of Music*

Esteban Buch's study of the "political history" of Beethoven's Ninth[1] is one of the very rare major attempts to address an ancient question: that of the relation between music and politics. Buch's approach is a historical one: After sketching out the "birth of modern political music" (the English "God Save the Queen" and the French "Marseillaise"), he follows the history of the reception of the "Ode to Joy" step by step, from its creation to the ups and downs of its fate in the twentieth century.

The transformations of this musical "object," however unique its extreme political appropriations may have been, are no less symptomatic. They are perhaps even exemplary of the aporias that threaten any discourse on music and its ideological or communitarian effects. In order to be convinced of this, one need only consider the very different values served by the Beethovenian "Ode to Joy" in recent history. And listen to the documents and testimonies gathered into a patient micrology in Esteban Buch's work.

1.

It was in 1951 that the adoption of the "Anthem of the Ninth Symphony" as the official European anthem was first proposed.[2] In effect, according to a secretary's report from the Council of Europe (the first European institution to be founded after the war in 1949), "The day that a European hymn salutes the European flag, as today the national hymn salutes the national flag in various countries, a great step will have been made along the road toward this essential union" (1950, 220). The need to turn to music for its *unifying* capacities. . . .

It is not until 1971, however, that another report (presented to the Consultative Assembly of the Council of Europe) recommends "the acceptance by member countries as a European anthem of *the Prelude to the Ode to Joy*," affirming that it is "preferable to select a musical work representative of European genius and whose use on European occasions *is already becoming something of a tradition*" (273, emphasis mine). We should immediately take note of the rudimentary articulation of a problem that will continue to concern us: This piece of music that, *from now on and for the future*, will be destined to serve a *new* symbolic function, to incarnate the spirit of a still embryonic institution, had to be *chosen*, it had to be *elected into this entirely novel role for the first time*, by virtue of the fact that it seemed to have *anticipated its own position*. We can call the strange temporality of musico-political invention *the paradox of the new anthem* that must first of all efface its novelty in order to institute the institution about which it sings in its *immediate eternity*. If one asks where and why such and such an anthem was invented, the anthem itself is perhaps essentially destined to have *both anticipated and prevented* any response.

The same 1971 report continues:

> As regards the words for an anthem, some doubt was felt, mainly with regard to the words of the Ode to Joy, which were in the nature of a universal expression of faith rather than specifically European. . . . Members also wondered whether any words acknowledged as "European" could ever be translated into another language and accepted as such by the other linguistic groups of the European family. . . . The committee therefore preferred, for the time being, to propose only the tune for a European anthem, without words, and to allow some time to pass. One day perhaps some words will be adopted by the citizens of Europe with the same *spontaneity* [emphasis mine] as Beethoven's eternal melody has been. (237–38)

Leaving aside the myth of an *anthemic spontaneity*—which reinforces the idea that such and such a song *will have from the beginning and always already been there in this role*—the report voices the very old topos of the universality of musical language, which, unlike plural and Babelian languages, would be above (or beneath) problems of translation. This is why, in a later 1973 report, the general secretary of the Council of Europe triumphantly claims, "In 1972 the Council of Europe gave Europeans a means of expressing their faith beyond the particularities of language" (242). The positive side of the equation is therefore the voice of peoples who commune in the harmonious affirmation of the values of universality and fraternity (*Alle Menschen werden Brüder* are the words to the "Ode to Joy" that continue to resound in spite of their absence).

2.

The negative side of the equation is, almost immediately, a sordid history of *copyright.* "The musical realization of the anthem has been entrusted to Mr. Herbert von Karajan," states a January 19, 1972, press release from the Council of Europe (cited 276). Karajan produces an *instrumental* arrangement of the piece to which he reserves the rights. Two years later, in 1974, the very same *Freudensmelodie* is adopted as the official hymn of the racist regime of Rhodesia (now Zimbabwe). As Buch puts it: "European was the term employed [in Rhodesia] to describe what was a political and social hegemony based on skin color [i.e., *apartheid*]. The anthem of the Rhodesian Europeans, too, was in a way a 'European anthem'" (244).

Several days after the announcement that the "Ode to Joy" was adopted as the Rhodesian anthem, the general secretary of the Council of Europe received a letter from the

French bureau of the European Veterans' Federation protesting against "the fact that the European anthem has become the anthem of apartheid" (247). The European institution will prove itself unable to sustain this protest in the name of the universalistic values of the Rights of Man; as an internal memo from the Office of Legal Affairs of the Council of Europe clearly states: "If Rhodesia has selected the 'Prelude to the Ode to Joy' in its original version, Rhodesia cannot be subject to reproach since that is a version that is in the public domain. If, on the other hand, Rhodesia has adopted the official score of the Council of Europe, no steps can be taken without the agreement of the person holding the copyright to that score, namely, Mr. Von Karajan" (245). Terrible irony of fate: the universal and fraternal *Freudensmelodie* could only have been saved from its racist misappropriation by a "former Nazi" (242). Yet because Rhodesia had only appropriated a work belonging to "the public domain and part of the universal cultural heritage," according to the words of the general secretary of the Council of Europe, this secretary responds to the group of veterans: "I understand your feelings, but I am afraid that in this matter no international recourse is available" (245).

3.

To what extent can one say of these accidents of history—which I am taking as exemplary of all those that have marked the long and sinister odyssey of the "Ode to Joy," beginning with the "era of nationalist movements" (156ff.), continuing with the darkest episodes of the Second World War (see "Beethoven as Führer," 201ff.) and lasting until today—to what extent can one say that they come *from the outside* to affect a piece of music that is supposed to incarnate *essentially* entirely different values? The question incessantly posed by Buch's study is, in effect, that of the *political responsibility internal to music.* Or, if one prefers, that of *a work's intrinsically political character.*

Considerations of the power of music are as old as the world, and considerations of its effects of transport or trance are of no use to us here. This is the case when Plato speaks of controlling music, of being careful that it serves the precise political ends attributed to it. When he recommends, for example, putting it into the exclusive service of courage and virtue by *excluding* its nostalgic or mollifying effects, he considers such effects as accomplished and recognized facts: Whether he accepts or refuses them is of little importance. He makes of them an *essential and unchangeable* property of specific modes or harmonies. "Which are the harmonies expressive of sorrow?" Socrates asks at one point (*Republic*, 398d–e). The answer: "The harmonies which you mean are the mixed Lydian and the bass Lydian, and such like." "And must not these harmonies be excluded?" Of course they must. And if they must, it is because it is inconceivable that the given modes could be instrumentalized for any function other than the one that *essentially* belongs to them.

This kind of musical *censorship* may seem naive to us because, as Adorno wrote in 1936, "it is radically impossible for us to experience the platonic characteristics of modes."[3] It should especially awaken a certain "suspicion" that Adorno mentions in this same letter to Ernst Krenek: "I have never been able to rid myself of the suspicion that the moral or calming effects that Plato assigns to different modes (which continue to haunt those critics who speak of a disquieting modern music and the like) were already in his own time speculative inventions, 'myths.'" In other words, these modal harmonies "owe their aura to the sole fact that they are taboo, and not to their eloquence."

The "Ode to Joy" from Beethoven's Ninth has never, to my knowledge, been the object of such a taboo. It has nonetheless certainly become a myth or a fetish. Yet for reasons that probably owe nothing to any censorship brought *from outside the work*. For the question here is not or is no longer whether or not the "Ode to Joy" is *essentially* the vehicle of one set of values or another. With Buch, we must rather consider that the "moral value" of Beethoven's music "cannot reasonably be based on the musical language itself." One must conclude that "musical language is either amoral or it expresses a notion of morality that includes tyrants—which is the same thing" (266).

Is there nothing then to be said or done? Must we then say that everything that has happened and will happen to the Ninth has nothing to do with the Ninth itself? That its changes, or rather the history of its reception, do not concern it? That in this case there is only a field of appropriative or disappropriative forces available for both the best and the worst?

4.

It is of course the case that any piece of music, whether or not it contains a "program" or clearly stated words, is subject to more or less disturbing appropriations, transplantations, or excerptions. As an example, one could cite Schoenberg's arrangement of Johann Strauss's famous "Emperor Waltz" (*Kaiserwalzer*) for a small ensemble (created in 1925 for the Society for Private Musical Performances). In his arrangement, Schoenberg couches veritable citations that function as glosses both on the waltz and on its title. Already in the seventh measure, by adding an accompaniment to the lyrical countermotif of the march, Schoenberg discreetly introduces a melody in the piano part that is none other than the theme from Haydn that now serves as the German national hymn, and which served in Austria as the "emperor's hymn" (*Kaiserhymne*) all the way through the very last years of the monarchy. With this somewhat subliminal citation of the hymn in the "Emperor Waltz," it is as if Schoenberg were also incorporating a commentary, words, in short an entire *discourse*, an eminently political one that perhaps coincided with Schoenberg's monarchist ideas.[4]

But to limit oneself to these wild appropriations that await any piece of music would imply using "pragmatism" as a pretext for reconstructing an *essentialist* vision of musical works, one that in spite of appearances to the contrary is only slightly different from Plato's. It would imply in particular that in spite of all that has been and might still happen to a work of music, the work "itself" remains intact and untouched. That all the "accidents" that can affect it do not change anything of the *essence* of the "Ode to Joy."

Faced with this apparent "pragmatism," which is one of the temptations of Buch's study, I prefer to follow another line of thought that he also suggests (in particular on page 107) about "the work's openness to being viewed as . . ." Alongside Buch, then, I will be looking for all possible clues that would suggest that the Ninth, "in and of itself," might have prepared the terrain and encouraged the possibilities of its most uncomfortable readings and appropriations.

5.

Buch writes (102) that, unlike Mozart and Haydn, who "freely blended their 'popular' melodies into the overall musical fabric of their works," Beethoven attempts to "emphasize the very different character of his *Freudenmelodie* in relation to the rest of the work."

> The narrative strategies he was to deploy to introduce, set forth, and develop a melody whose very structure makes it a self-contained whole, an independent musical object, were to play a decisive role in the symphony's interpretation. . . . The duality between the autonomy of the "joy melody" and its structural role in the fourth movement reflects the differing interpretations which, in the history of the Ninth's reception, have served either to emphasize the theme's role as a communal anthem for the public arena or to view it solely as one integral and concrete element in a total work of pure music.

What are these strategies and what is this duality?

We know that the introduction to the Ninth's finale, before it breaks into the "Ode to Joy," presents successive citations of the preceding movements. These form something like windows open onto the work's past, windows just as quickly closed with the intervention of an "instrumental recitative" in the cellos and double basses, who seem to be saying, "No, this is not the music we want any more; we are looking for something else; we are in search of the hymn you are going to hear." Here more than ever, Beethoven's musical writing seems to be aiming for a system of listening that presupposes the listener's *own identification* with the creator so that the listener can follow the genesis of the work *step by step*. As Edward Dannreuther wrote in 1876, in an article that helped construct the myth of the composer-prophet:

> [Beethoven] frequently chooses to put together his material in the presence of the listener as it were. He gives part of his thought first—a rhythmical phrase perhaps—a single point, a few chords, rests, and the like, which he gradually widens, strengthens and enforces, until from the entire movement an idea of the whole detaches itself, that the hearer is allowed to see in the light of a flower-crowned plant, of which the whole course of growth, from a simple germ to its final glory, is visible at one glance.[5]

If the "Ode to Joy" is the "flower" of the Ninth, the question we need to ask is as follows: To what extent is it possible to *cut* a flower, to pluck and conserve it, to transplant it and make it into an emblem or a flag? Or, more precisely: To what extent has the work *itself* (the "plant") prepared and inspired its cut?[6]

To understand the detail of the veritable *staging*, within the work, *of its own genesis*, Buch carefully considers "some particularly pertinent verbal evidence of Beethoven's creative process" during the Ninth conserved in the famous Beethoven sketchbooks.

> The composer's words at times seem to be rough sketches for some sung text and at others merely comments by the composer, it is not always possible to tell which. Thus, Beethoven entered in his notebook an introductory fanfare in C major, followed by a few notes of a recitative. . . . Over the first phrase of the recitative, Beethoven wrote: "*Nein diese erinnern an unsre Verzweifl*" [No, that would remind us of our despair]. In the same manner, he selected the texts for each of the recitatives that follow the quotations of the prior movements, each phrase serving

to justify the rejection of the melody quoted. And at the end of the series, we find the "joy" theme, followed by a long melisma and the note: "*Ha dieses ist es. Es ist nun gefunden Freu*" [Ah! here it is! It's been found]. Then Beethoven wrote: "*Lasst uns das Lied der unsterblichen Schiller singen*"—"Let us sing the immortal Schiller's song!" The sequence of sketches narrates a thematic search . . . of reasoned rejections of preceding melodies until the *Freudensmelodie* at last appears—rejections that define, a contrario, the characteristics of the latter. . . . The instrumental portion of the symphony is the domain of the possible melodies from which the communal song will emerge—for if the "joy melody" appears to be introduced as the contradiction of the preceding movements, it is at the same time anticipated in certain passages of these movements (especially in the Trio of the Scherzo). The "discovery" of the theme, therefore, is the telos of a twofold quest, one strictly musical and ongoing throughout the symphony, and the other metadiscursive, in which the symphony itself, through the soloist, announces the "replacement" of those thematic materials by the new melody. The baritone is both the actor in this quest and the master of ceremonies at a "fete" that will consist in a unison singing of the anthem—Schiller's lied. (102–3)

In the final version of the Ninth, something of this genesis does indeed remain, "as the soloist exhorts his 'friends' to abandon the preceding melodies and to sing the melody of joy" (103). The baritone's famous words, "*O Freunde! Nicht diese Tone! Sondern lasst uns angenehmere anstimmen und freudenvollere!*" (O friends, not those sounds! Rather let us sing a more agreeable and more joyous song!) are

Beethoven's (not Schiller's), and it is through them that the "'different' character of the *Freudenmelodie*" is "dramatized *in the work itself*" (ibid., emphasis added). Must we then conclude, as Buch does, that "the work's openness to being viewed as a narrative" contributes to the explanation of "the process that entails extracting the 'Ode to Joy' from its symbolic ritual context" (the genesis of the work) "and transferring it onto a virtual ritual as a musical symbol for a political community"?

6.

In this case, Beethoven will no doubt have dramatized, and more than ever before, the *cutting of the flower*. By making the work into the *theater of its own representation*, he will have opened the abyssal border of a *stage*: as if the work were attending itself, paying homage to itself with a crown of flowers, *commemorating itself.*

But this Beethovenian gesture is even more ambiguous and paradoxical than Buch's study suggests: Is not this staging of the self-engendering of the work-plant, this *autogeneration*, is it not *also* the most powerful way to tighten the ties between the four movements of the Ninth and to prevent its being crumbled into "chosen pieces" detached from the great corpus of the work considered as an organism? In the history of symphonic music, there are many examples of this type of process (which musicologists call "cyclic") where the repetition of themes from earlier movements is meant to ensure the *unity* of a much larger composition.

Contrary to Buch's apparent affirmation, what he calls "the duality between the autonomy of the 'joy melody' and its structural role in the fourth movement," *this* duality between the friability or atomization of the work on the one hand and organic dependency on the other, this *duality* certainly proves itself to be *undecidable* in terms of its "internal" or "external" status. For if we maintain that it is the "work" that, "structurally" and from its "interior," would prescribe and thus write in advance the history of its reception as a *dismemberment*, what meaning could we thereby find in notions of "interiority," "structure," "organicity," and so on?

One can still consider that the political effects grafted from or forced onto the "Ode to Joy" have nothing *musical* about them. As Rousseau writes in his *Dictionary of Music* about the "Ranz des vaches" that would so often upset Swiss soldiers, one can think that "these effects . . . come solely from habit, from memories, from a thousand circumstances which, recounted by this Tune to those who hear it and recalling for them their country, their old pleasures, their youth, and all their ways of living, arouse in them a bitter pain for having lost all that," in short, that "*Music* therefore does not precisely act as *Music*, but as a memorative sign."[7] The question nonetheless remains unanswered in the very particular case of the Ninth, because Beethoven will have attempted to inscribe this "memorative sign" *into the music itself*, to make of it *a memory of the work and within the work.*

The reception of a work, as the terminology goes, or the open entirety of its active arrangements and derangements, is perhaps always a form of violence in terms of an organicist or "structural" conception of "The Work." Once one accepts this premise, one can consider that the Ninth, by claiming to inscribe its own becoming and its own history into its "structure," will have heightened the risk or desire for its appropriation as a radical disappropriation, exasperating it for centuries to come. By wanting to make of the "hymn" the fable of the work's telos, as if it had *always already* been the *intrinsic* aim of the work, Beethoven, even as he gave unheard of force to his *autogenetic fiction* (even as he lent an unprecedented theatrical power to the organicist ideal of the work), will have perhaps unleashed in advance the worst kinds of violence from another stage: that of the *fiction of the political.* In other words, the "metadiscursive" character (as Buch puts it), or the *hyperbolical mastery* toward which Beethoven's discourse tends in the Ninth, is reversed into absolute dispossession.

Right from the beginning, right from its first sketches, the "Ode to Joy" will have preceded itself in a fabulous staging (or mise en abyme) of its own origin. And this is perhaps why it has been and continues to be so *disposed* to traffic in all kinds of symbols.

P.S. (June 2000)

After the debate following the conference, a contrast became clear to me: the contrast between what I called the Beethovenian cut into the Ninth's finale and the breakthrough that Adorno analyzed in Mahler's First Symphony. This overly summary postscriptum simply attempts to situate some of the stakes of a contrast that will need further development.

If there has ever been a musical thinking about the politics in and of music, it is certainly that of Adorno. The idea that the very "material" of musicians is coursed through with the political is sensible everywhere in his work. This is particularly true of his 1960 Mahler study,[8] where he declares: "If Mahler's development as a composer mediates between the world's course and that which is other, the mediation, in order to go deep enough, should be detectable *in the substance of his music itself*" (14, emphasis added).

One of the major figures for this mediation is the one Adorno, in the very first pages of his book, calls a *breakthrough*: "What the immanence of society blocks cannot be achieved by an immanence of form derived from it. The breakthrough sought to penetrate both" (6).

Without being able to pursue as one should the notions of "matter" and "form" in Adorno's work (a subject that would demand very lengthy study), I would simply remark that the figure of the breakthrough, placed as it is at the opening of *Mahler*, bears in an exemplary way the promise of a utopian force inscribed in music itself: This is not, like the cut of the Ninth, the moment when so-called "pure" (instrumental) music opens itself up to voice, to text, or to a discursive program that could be called "extramusical." No, the breakthrough is rather the moment when the elements of a formal logic internal to music seem subtracted from their expected consequences, the better to dig into the work the abyss of the promise of a better world.

In the first movement of the First Symphony, this breakthrough is described by Adorno in the following way:

> The First Symphony opens with a long pedal point in the strings. . . . A thin curtain, threadbare but densely woven, it hangs from the sky like a pale gray cloud layer, similarly painful to sensitive eyes. In the third measure the motive of a fourth detaches itself, tinged by the piccolo. . . . After a second woodwind entry, the motive of the fourth descends sequentially until it comes to rest on a B-flat that clashes with the A of the strings. The tempo suddenly quickens with a pianissimo fanfare for two clarinets in their pale, lower register, with the weak bass clarinet as

> the third voice, sounding faintly as if from behind the curtain that it vainly seeks to penetrate, its strength failing. Even when the fanfare is taken up by the trumpets it still remains, as the score directs, *in sehr weiter Entfernung* [in the far distance]. Then, at the height of the movement, six measures before the return of the tonic D, the fanfare explodes in the trumpets, horns, and high woodwinds, quite out of scale with the orchestra's previous sound or even the preceding crescendo. It is not so much that this crescendo has reached a climax as that the music has expanded with a physical jolt. The rupture originates from beyond the music's intrinsic movement, intervening from outside. For a few moments the symphony imagines that something has become reality that for a lifetime the gaze from the earth has fearfully yearned for in the sky. . . . If all music, with its first note, promises that which is different, the rending of the veil, his symphonies attempt to withhold it no longer, to place it literally before our eyes. (4–5)

In coldly "technical" terms, the breakthrough would therefore be a kind of disproportion between what the beginning of the movement promised and allowed us to expect and what, to the contrary, the return of this beginning in the final measures allows to explode without warning, without common measure to what any common musical measure would have allowed us to anticipate. The breakthrough would therefore be the rupture of a certain promise—let's say: the promise of a form[9]—as a way of better allowing an entirely different promise to be pronounced: the promise that precisely because it escapes the expectations inscribed into forms, promises the *entirely other*.

For Adorno, the promise the breakthrough bears of what is entirely other seems entirely incompatible with its inscription in a form. In other words, in a work of art.

> The idea of breakthrough, which dictates the entire structure of the movement, transcends the traditional form while fleetingly sketching its outline.
>
> But Mahler's primary experience, inimical to art, needs art in order to manifest itself. . . . (6)
>
> The artistic obligation that occasioned his aversion to the redundancies of the program constrains him to elaborate the breakthrough in strictly musical terms, to shed his naive hostility to art, until the breakthrough itself becomes an intrinsic element of form. However, his concept is not inviolable. It is in the logic of composition to criticize what it seeks to represent; the more achieved the work, the poorer grows hope, for hope seeks to transcend the finitude of the harmoniously self-sufficient work. . . . It is doubtful, in view of the rift between the world's course and that which is other, whether there is more truth where that Other is manifested without pretense that the subject attains realization through the work . . . or where the internal coherence of the work simulates a coherence of meaning, insisting on its own truth, only to become in its entirety a deception. (11)

The question Adorno leaves us with is, therefore, as follows: How can the work be a promise even though its nature as a work turns this promise into a false hope? And what does "truth" become—the "truth content," the *Wahrheitsgehalt* so dear to Adorno—once its inscription in a form or into a material[10] turns it into a potential lie? What still awaits us, in music, is a thinking of the unworkability (*désoeuvrement*) of and within the work, beyond even those passages where Adorno speaks of works as "problems."[11] And to the extent that Adornian "aesthetics" are perhaps musical above all else, one should no doubt begin a deconstruction of his notion of the work in the perspective of a resistance that music, more than literature, opposes to the idea of an inoperable community.[12]

CHAPTER 7 Da Capo: *Follow the Notes*

Wednesday, December 24

Do you remember the end and those last images?[1]

After the tragic events that shook the orchestra, the concert hall is in ruins. Surrounded by a cloud of dust, amid the rubble from which the inert body of the harpist has been removed, the conductor gets up and slowly speaks, his words interrupted by long pauses; in his poor Italian with its German accent, he quietly says:

> You are here, I am here. . . . We must each pay attention to our instrument. This is all we can do, now.[2]

In a low voice, he tells the percussionist who is helping him put his music stand back up: "The notes us save. Music us save." (*Le note salvano noi. La musica salva noi.*) Then, turning to the other musicians who are gathering around, already holding their instruments, he instructs them:

> Stick to the notes. Follow the notes. One by one. As my hands will show you. We are musicians. You are musicians. We are here to try again. Have no fear. The rehearsal goes on. Resume your places, gentlemen. Back in place, please.[3]

And the orchestra starts up again, just as instructed. It plays the piece all the way through, and then stops. The conductor once again speaks, this time in another tone of voice that slowly mounts into an eruption of violence.

> We must give to sounds a little less color. Perhaps it is good to remember that noise is not music. . . . Where are we here? On a football field? Do you maybe think I am a referee? And those winds, where are you? What are you doing? What is happening with your little lungs? Where has your breath gone? Lost in your idiotic chatter?[4]

At this point, the screen goes black, and the conductor switches from Italian to German, screaming:

> Breathe with might! *Mit Kraft!* The trumpets have to wake the dead! . . . Are you musicians or not? I want a sound that has the color of fire! Gentlemen, *da capo*![5]

The music starts up again as the credits to the film appear on the black screen. This is a description of the last minutes of *Prova d'orchestra*, an "orchestra rehearsal" filmed by Fellini with music by Nino Rota.[6]

Thursday, December 25

"Stick to the notes," he said. "Follow the notes. One by one."

I would have liked to write a treatise for you, to compile an encyclopedia of the infinite occurrences and resonances of those three short phrases in the vast archive of the history of musical power. But I know I won't be able to. I'm too distracted. I end up indulging in stories, or in being told tales.

It is true that among the tales and legends that come to distract me from my encyclopedic pretensions, I occasionally find some that are about the power of music. What I call its power of *duction*, or its power to take us away.

As a matter of fact, following these stories rather than the notes themselves, I might actually be able to tell you a bit about these several phrases from the conductor. But also about the strange and certainly frightening region to which they may lead—if they lead anywhere at all, to anything that could even be called a place.

One thing is certain: The conductor *conducts.* He is the *conducteur*, or the driver, as Berlioz still referred to him in his 1855 treatise (*Le chef d'orchestre: Théorie de son art*), and he is still called this today in English. I have already tried to describe elsewhere how he conducts or drives,[7] and I would now like to at least try to know where in the world he might lead us. Both he and all those who like him have some kind of a grasp on the power of musical duction.

Where are we going, with music? Do you happen to know?

Friday, December 26

So I gave in to my indulgence. Tonight, the two crafty ones who didn't want to sleep convinced me that I should tell them a story. I don't know who wrote it, and for good reason: It's a legend that they chose—a legend that, like all legends, begins with that old undated incipit: "Once upon a time . . ."

Later on, after looking, I found that there are many written versions of the fabulous tale of *The Pied Piper of Hamelin* in German and in English. If one believes the version collected by the brothers Grimm in their *Deutsche Sagen* (1818), the legend describes an event that occurred in the city of Hamelin at the end of the thirteenth century.

> The year of 1284 saw a strange man come to Hamelin. He had a coat made out of a multicolored patchwork cloth. . . . He introduced himself as a ratcatcher [*Rattenfänger*] and, for a given amount of money, promised to free the city of its mice and rats. The citizens came to an agreement with him and promised him a certain salary. The ratcatcher took out a pipe and whistled into it [*pfiff*]: the rats and mice came crawling out of all the houses and gathered together around him [*sammelten sich um ihn herum*]. The moment he thought that none remained behind [*es wäre keine zurück*], he came out, and the whole lot followed him, and this is how he drove them to the Weser [*und der ganze Haufen folgte ihm, und so führte er sie an die Weser*]; there, he rolled up his clothes and went into the water, at which point all the animals followed him [*worauf ihm alle die Tiere folgten*] and drowned themselves by diving. (*Die Kinder zu Hameln*, translation mine)

I find myself dreaming while I read, while they listen to me as they fall asleep. I hear my voice telling them these words—follow, drive—and they inevitably call to mind *Prova d'orchestra*. "Follow the notes": Isn't that the precise injunction tacitly accompanying the sounds of the pipe through the streets of Hamelin?

As you certainly know, the tale does not end there. Over the course of the legend, there is a kind of repetition, a *da capo*: after the rats and the mice, the children. As the brothers Grimm recount it:

After the citizens were freed of their torment, they regretted having promised the salary and refused to pay the man using all sorts of excuses, and he left angry and bitter. On June 26, the day of John and Paul, at seven in the morning—or, according to others, at noon—he reappeared, this time as a hunter, with a frightening face and a strange red hat, and he started playing his pipe in the streets. This time, it was not the rats and mice that came, but many, many children. . . . The whole swarm followed him, and he drove it to a mountain [*der ganze Schwarm folgte ihm nach, und er führte sie hinaus in einen Berg*], into which he disappeared with them. . . . All one hundred thirty of them were lost. According to what some have said, two of them were late and came back; but one of these was blind and the other mute: the blind one could not show where the place was, but is said to have told of how they had followed the piper; the mute one could have showed where they were, but without having heard anything. A little boy had left in only a shirt and had turned around to get his coat, thus escaping the misfortune. for when he came back, the others had already disappeared behind a hill, which people still point out. (Ibid.)

Da capo, it all starts over: The piper reappears; he comes back in the guise of a hunter. It's because he has not been paid that he returns to Hamelin, to seduce, or to divert (in German, *verführen*), the children of the city. And, once again, he leads them, he drives them (*führt*) with the sound of his pipe.

This time, there are indeed survivors. And these survivors *could have been* witnesses; They *could have been able* to recount. But, because they were deaf, mute, or blind, they either couldn't see or couldn't hear anything, and they thus cannot tell the whole story. As for the last little one, the one who made the trip back to get something to cover himself up, he simply missed out on the scene.

In this first version of the legend, we know very little: nothing about the music, nothing about the hidden causes of its ductive powers, nothing about the circumstances of the disappearance that it brings about. Another version was also collected by the brothers Grimm ("Der Rattenfänger"), but it hardly says much more.

> The ratcatcher knows a certain note [*einen gewissen Ton*]; if he whistles it nine times, all the rats follow after him [*pfeift er den neunmal, so ziehen ihm alle Ratten nach*] to where he wants to take them, into the pond or the pool.

Why such restraint, why such a resistance to saying anything about the sounds of the piper? Why make the possible witnesses incapable of witnessing? Or rather: Why does music, whenever it is a question of its capacity for duction or for seduction, always seem to forbid any form of testimony about it? Does one's subjection to music presuppose its allegedly ineffable or unspeakable nature?

Saturday, December 27

Yet again tonight, they wanted me to start over. For me to tell the same story again, *da capo*. So I did.

Then, later on, when I was alone, I read the most extensive (and most famous) version of this legend: the adaptation in verse rendered by Robert Browning (*The Pied Piper of Hamelin*, published in 1888). And in it, on the subject of the pipe and the music that comes from it, I found several imagined details that provide counterpoint to the sounds of the animal crowd on the march.

> And ere three shrill notes the pipe uttered,/You heard as if an army muttered;/And the muttering grew to a grumbling;/And the grumbling grew to a mighty rumbling;/and out of the house the rats came tumbling.

In addition, because here, unlike in the Grimms' version, there is a survivor among the beasts, one can read testimony to what, after the simple signal of the three initial notes, will continue to resound until the moment the crowd reaches the mountain. It is actually a rat, "stout as Julius Caesar," who sets down the scene in writing (in "the manuscript he cherished," as Browning puts it). And this writing rat "lived to carry . . ./To Rat-land home his commentary."

His survivor's tale is a description of a paradisiacal world, where visions of abundance ("apples, wondrous ripe . . .") are conjured by an enchanting voice.

> And it seemed as if a voice/(Sweeter far than by harp or by psaltery/Is breathed) called out. Oh rats, rejoice!/The world is grown to one vast drysaltery!

In Browning's version, there is a desire to accentuate the repetitive character of the legend: In order for the *da capo* to be even more stringently followed, the sole survivor among the rats has a corresponding figure in the single witness among the children. It's a little limping child, who, because he was late, was unable to start the climb up the mountain. Yet he says nothing about the music—to which only an animal will, in the final analysis, have testified, however little. The limping child tells only the music's message—in other words, the promise that is transmitted by the notes that give voice to it.

> For he led us, he said, to a joyous land,/Joining the town and just at hand,/Where . . . everything was strange and new.

With or without voice, playing a pipe, or—as in Goethe's poetic version called *Der Rattenfänger*—acting through "magical strings and song" (*bei Zaubersaiten und Gesang*), the ratcatcher is certainly a prosopopeia of music and its power to take us away. But music, quite precisely, tends to efface itself each time behind the mask that personifies it. Strangely, it almost disappears from the legend as soon as it appears. It actually only ever appears as music *in general*; it indifferentiates itself to the point of being no more than a kind of voice in the service of an imperative that commands by promising something. This makes its capacity to seduce appear related to what is said and announced, beyond or beneath the notes. Music acts in the service of a message (it proclaims both the existence of a better world and its own ability to lead to it). Music submits itself to a saying (a saying that is perhaps beyond the sayable). By carrying itself away toward this diction, it seems to gain its power of duction. But only when it sacrifices its own differentiation, when it loses any characteristic musical mark.

Music itself, then, is what drives the rats and the children, music itself in all the abrupt power of its generality; what carries them away as a mass is, massively, music itself, which claims the existence of an elsewhere by proclaiming itself music, music in general, music as music.

Does this then mean that it is only by losing itself, by diving into the funnel of a general loudspeaker where it becomes indifferent, that music, hence destined to an almost *amusical* indistinction, would gain all the ductive powers attributed to it?

Sunday, December 28

Tonight, I am alone. And it is to myself alone that the legend of the piper comes back—*da capo*—itself consisting in ghostly returns and repetitions. It comes back to me, though, in another of its forms: the variant that Brecht gave of it and that he calls, precisely as a way of marking its difference from all the other variants, *Die* wahre *Geschichte vom Rattenfänger von Hameln*; in other words (with my emphasis): "the *true* story of the ratcatcher from Hamelin."

It's a poem in verse with a simple, popular tone: almost a song like those sung by the vagabonds and beggars in *The Threepenny Opera*. The last two lines of each stanza are identical. They come back in a rhymed refrain: "He whistled well. He whistled long./'Twas certainly a surprising song." (*Er pfiff hübsch. Er pfiff lang./'s war ein wunderbarer Klang.*)

Among the recurrences of this refrain that weaves its way through the narrative, what is so different about this version? What gives it the right to the qualifying *true* of the title? Why is it that it can claim to state, among the innumerable adaptations of the legend, the truth presumably hidden in all the other versions?

Taking a distance from previous versions, Brecht simplifies things; he takes out the episode with the rats in favor of going straight to the point, right in the first stanza: the abduction of the children.

> The ratcatcher from Hamelin/Came right into town/With his pipe he got them/All the children, all the thousand.[8]

The second stanza, in an apparently analogous way to Browning's, presents the duction or the seduction by music as the promise of a better world; yet this promise is not a ruse. Brecht portrays it as an attempt at emancipation.

> The ratcatcher from Hamelin/From the town would like to save them/So that growing up/They might find a haven./He whistled well. He whistled long./'Twas certainly a surprising song.[9]

But the real *coup de theatre* Brecht introduces into the legend intervenes in the fourth and fifth stanzas (the only ones, in fact, whose rhymed refrain changes).

> The ratcatcher from Hamelin/When he left the town/They say his whistling/Chained his own senses down/I whistle well. I whistle long./'Tis truly a surprising song.// The ratcatcher from Hamelin/Rode around the mountain/And into the town by mistake/Brought the children back again./Whistled too well. Whistled too long./It was just too surprising a song.

In the space of a second, we go from the distant and external voice of the narrator to the voice of the piper himself, who says "I" here. And once it is he himself who speaks, the story gains an additional fold. The narrative folds in on itself: The driver himself is driven, seduced; he is driven by the driving force that he had nonetheless seemed to master. In short, the transitivity of musical duction becomes reflexivity. This means that this music that seemed to drive or carry toward the promise of otherness or of elsewhere brings us back to the circularity of the selfsame. Musical sovereignty, the sovereign force of music's duction, gets carried away into the circle of its power.

All of this makes it seem as if, with this reflexive, perhaps even self-referential buckling, music begins to turn on itself, and to make all those it was supposed to lead elsewhere turn in circles. Forgetting his goal, his objective and his end, the piper goes all the way around the mountain and returns to the town. This is so much the case that music, all of a sudden, seems to be untethered from the finality that brought it beyond itself, and which brought the crowd to follow along behind it, by driving and mobilizing the crowd. In the circle Brecht draws it into, music is not far from becoming absolute music, pure and detached from any foreign finality, buckled onto itself in the auto-referential figure of the circle.

Sunday, January 4

I happen to know that Fellini was suspicious of music. I just found confirmation of this fact in that book I found when I was with you.[10] In an interview with the singer Lucio Dalla, he speaks of music as an "invasion" (*invasione*) and he says:

> Starting in my early childhood, music created within me a dimension of profound melancholy. It's something I have to defend myself against. . . . [M]usic gives you back the weight and miserable nature of your situation [*la miserabilità della tua situazione*] in a continuous blackmail [*ricatto*]: the allusion to something more perfect and more harmonious, something you are excluded from.

Music, Fellini says, sings and makes you sing. It blackmails you.[11] Like its prosopopeia in the guise of a piper, it promises or wields the promise of an infinitely consoling elsewhere even as it immediately closes that elsewhere off into the confines of silence. It promises an escape to happiness even as it forbids anyone to witness it. It is jealous, exclusive, perhaps even vengeful. And its blackmail [*chantage*]—that promise within reach that it takes away by leaving only silence behind it—is infinitely repeated, *da capo*.

For, as Fellini further eloquently suggests, with music, *every time seems like the last time.*

> I am convinced that if, at the end of our life, we were allowed to say something, and if we were truly sincere, we would sing a little ditty as a summary of an entire existence [*come riassunto di tutta un'esistenza*]. I realize this when I consider four or five motifs that always invade me with the same nostalgia, the same emotion, the same regret [*la stessa nostalgia, commozione, lo stesso rimpianato*]. (Ibid.)

Every time music comes back, it seems to say that this time is the last time. Each time, it brings with it the regret of what would be ultimate, a kind of ultimatum or summation that would say: Here it is, after all, what will have been and what will never be again. As if in each one of its recurrences, at each of its *da capo*'s, music presented itself as the ultimate witness of a (past or future) world to which one cannot testify in turn.

Every time it comes back and presents itself again, music is accompanied by an "I was there" that makes that elsewhere sing in order to blackmail us with it. "I was there," *io c'ero*, Fellini in fact wrote in his notes for a musical film he never shot;[12] and his words say what returning music always says or makes us say.

> I was there [*io c'ero*]! Times past. Faraway eras . . . I remember it very well, I see them. I was there, I have always been there [*io c'ero, ci sono sempre stato*].

The "I" in this "I was there" cries tears and is regretful. It *recries*, as I would be tempted to translate that untranslatable Italian verb, *rimpiangere*, whose object is being interrogated by Fellini.

What does music make us mourn, deplore, regret, or recry, he asks Lucio Dalla? Dalla gives this astounding answer:

> Music certainly does not make me mourn what was [*rimpiangere quello che è stato*]. It makes me mourn what has *not* been [*rimpiangere quello che* non *è stato*], the great and profound melancholy that ties me to things I have not lived [*la grande, profonda malinconia che mi lega alle cosec he non ho vissuto*].

Must we therefore consider that music, when it says or makes us say "I was there" (*io c'ero*), etches a lack in advance into the pronoun indicating whatever place it may be—a lack or an absence, a kind of necessary ban or banishment? Can we consider that the distance affecting the "I was there"—affecting it with affects and with regrets and with tears—is not only a temporal distance in relation to a past that has become remote or in relation to a future that has merely been glimpsed, but also, but rather and before, a gap in presence itself, at the very heart of past, present, or future presence?

In music as music, that which sings and makes us sing, blackmailing us, would therefore be that voice without voice that seems in advance to dig out the abyss of an exile into the heart of asylum.

Wednesday, January 7

Today, in the train that drives me and takes me away at high speed toward my destination, I think once again of *Prova d'orchestra*.

The entire film takes place indoors. The only moment we hear noises from outside the former oratory that serves as a room for the orchestra's rehearsals, without seeing anything at all, is during the opening credits, with its horns, sirens, and screeching tires—in short, sounds that come from an outside that is implicitly opposed to music and to the enclosure where music is produced. All the rest of the film is confined to the oratory devoted to rehearsal. Almost all of it, at least.

Toward the end of the film, the enclosed space of the film is cracked open. The oratory's wall is smashed in by a huge steel ball, like the balls used for demolition. This irruption from the outside is also an interruption. It brings the series of crises traversed by the orchestra to a halt and brings to an end the sequence of these situations that are also political allegories:[13] the despotism of the conductor, the trade unionism or parliamentarianism of the musicians, the revolution or anarchy that calls for the abolition of all power . . .

Yet what makes the conclusion of the film so gripping, and so terrifying, is that through the force of duction incarnated by the conductor, music seems to be able to close up the breach in the wall in spite of everything: The wall has indeed fallen down and brought about the death of the harpist, leaving a landscape of ruin and debris. But the conductor, the *direttore,* takes up his baton, reiterates the injunction to follow the notes, and it all starts up again. After the revolution, music will have brought things around again. A return to the initial situation, a return to the (capital) principle of authoritarian conduction, a return to the conductor, and a reversal of course: *da capo.*

The legend of the pied piper of Hamelin has a strikingly symmetrical structure, even if it is partly inversed. The story takes place in the outdoors, outside, in the streets of the city and the fields around it. And it leads, musically speaking, to the slope of the mountain, which closes in upon itself to confine the children in the enclosure of a dreamed-for promise, which, it would seem, they will never escape.

In the version transmitted by the brothers Grimm, as in Robert Browning's, this capture or enclosure through and in music is commemorated by the institution of a new calendar, inaugurating within the city a cycle in which the misfortunes of musical duction or abduction are infinitely repeated as if in an echo.

> The citizens of Hamelin had the event inscribed into the register of their city and took care to count the years and the days of their acts according to the loss of their children. (Brothers Grimm, *Die Kinder zu Hameln*)

Commemorative inscriptions also reiterate the event—on the wall of the town hall and on the new gate to the city. Then, still according to the brothers Grimm, almost three centuries later, in 1572, they had the story "represented in the church's stained glass" and minted into coins that cited the event. Finally, the musical capacity that caused the catastrophe was also remembered and reproduced in reverse, as a negative, in the prohibition it inspired. According to the Brothers Grimm,

> the street the children took to get to the gate was, in the middle of the eighteenth century (and probably still today), still called the *bunge-lose* [without drum, without sound, silent], for no dance was to be danced there, and no string instrument plucked.[14]

From within its own plotline, the legend thus already repeats and inscribes itself everywhere, right into the calendar that will forever mark any future event. *Da capo.*

It would therefore seem that in this story, music's effect is, as one says in French, to *open the ban, ouvrir le ban*; it brings about the proclamation of a new order, with its edicts and its prohibitions.

Friday, January 9

I've already told you about my brief—and nonetheless overly long—venture into military music. From it, I remember in particular that expression: *ouvrir le ban*, which designates the drum roll that precedes the proclamation of an order or a prize-giving ceremony.

In the complex and dense lexical family of which the word "*ban*" has been the source, one finds banality and abandon, as well as banishment.

Certain historians, commentators, and adaptors of the legend of the pied piper have seen in the story a transposition of the banishment declared on children infected with the plague. Others—the Brothers Grimm, for example, or Browning—have suggested a reading based on voluntary and collective exile: an emigration. The Grimms write: "Some say that the children were led into a cavern and came out of it in Siebenbürgen." Browning completes this hypothesis:

> And I must not omit to say/That in Transylvania there's a tribe/Of alien people that ascribe/The outlandish ways and dress/On which their neighbors lay such stress,/To their fathers and mothers having risen/Out of some subterraneous prison/Into which they were trepanned.

Without even saying anything about banality in this affair (I'll tell you about that another time, in relation to another story of chant and mouse as told by Kafka), tonight, I simply wonder: What ties the ban, along with banishment and its varied related forms (exile and emigration) to abandonment, to the movement that consists in abandoning oneself to music and to its capacity for duction, to its violence? And about that violence: Is it, precisely—to reconsider a distinction Benjamin formulated in his 1921 "Critique of Violence"[15]—"law-making" or "law-preserving"? Or should we instead try, yet again following Benjamin's lead, to understand musical violence not as a means to whatever kind of an end, but as detached from any finality, as "nonmediate"? Should we think of it as analogous to "anger," about which Benjamin declares that it manifests and presents "the most visible outbursts of a violence that is not related as a means to a preconceived end"?[16]

Saturday, January 10

I've already spoken to you about music and its promises, about its spaces and its distances, about its blackmail and its singing, about the threat that accompanies it and that seems every time to make it say it's the last time.

That was a year ago now.

That was a whole other story, a very short story that read a lot like a fable. There were already mice in that one. And the narrator wondered about the strange power of a kind of music that may have had nothing musical about it, so banal and indifferent did it seem. All while presenting itself as music itself: music *as* music.

A year ago, I was telling you that short tale as a way of telling you about us. Today, it seems both so old and so new to me, a new-old short story in which the unheard-of still resonates.

So here yet again, *da capo*, are those letters in which I spoke to you about a certain Josephine, a singer, in the land of mice. Tonight, I smile as I reread them.

CHAPTER 8 *Kafka at the* Star Academy: *Nothing's Anthem*

I had a dream during a recent trip to Rome.[1]

I had to sing on a stage like the *Star Academy*'s, and my vocal performance was going to be judged. I was told that I was below a first quantifiable cut-off point because my voice didn't carry. This actually came as no surprise.

But, I was further told and this time to my great surprise, I was also beneath a second cut-off point: the one needed in order to *feel oneself* sing or speak, in other words to *hear oneself* speak or sing. I was told that I would not be able to hear myself, as if my voice were condemned to remain a prisoner in my deaf inner room. I could shout myself hoarse, the judges insisted, but my voice would remain without voice, and already and above all else for myself.

When I woke up disturbed by this dream, I immediately thought of Josephine.

Josephine, yes, the heroine of a short story by Kafka that reads like a fable: "Josephine the Singer, or the Mouse Folk."[2] It's a kind of legend concerning the powers of music and voice. Josephine, as we will see, has an immense power over the "folk" that listen to her. Even if, or perhaps precisely because, she apparently has no voice.

What we are going to try to read, then, is this "mere nothing in voice" (367), as the narrator puts it, which nonetheless seems to have extensive power over an entire people that does indeed listen to her. It's "this nothing concerning the voice" (*dieses Nichts an Stimme*), a voice so banal and ordinary that it resembles all other voices, all our voices, and is nonetheless, within its very banality, marked as an exception, to the point of incarnating the *raison d'être* of a public that exists only through and for her.

"Our singer is called Josephine."

The story's first sentence immediately names the eponymous character of the story: Josephine, fragility itself, a kind of weak little organism faced with a people whose rigidly enclosed organization makes it seem pitiless.

If the banal discretion of this incipit does not at first seem remarkable, it nonetheless quickly becomes so. The first two words, in particular, start to tremble.

"Our," first of all (*unsere*).

The possessive becomes strange, with the sharing it presupposes but which the narrative immediately contradicts, for the *we* at stake here, this collective that seems to assemble an entire people, is a *we* that is entirely foreign to that which it appears to possess. Josephine is indeed a musician, but the people are not: "We are not in general a music-loving race," says the narrator, and he adds a bit further on that Josephine is "the only one" (*die einzige*) who "has a love for music and knows too how to transmit it."

Because they are so preoccupied by their daily tasks, the mice apparently do not have access to the faraway world music represents.

> Our life is hard; we are no longer, even on occasions when we have tried to shake off the cares of daily life, to

rise to anything so high and remote from our usual routine as music.

Music is almost presented as a kind of evil or misfortune, perhaps in proportion to the promise of distant bliss it incarnates and offers as a faraway temptation in contrast to banality. When the narrator explains that the mice benefit from "a certain practical cunning" that allows them "to console [them]selves for everything," and that their survival depends on this characteristic, he also adds this strange qualification:

> even supposing—only it has not happened—that we were to yearn once in a way for the kind of bliss which music may provide . . . [*auch wenn wir einmal—was aber nicht geschieht—das Verlangen nach dem Glück haben sollten, das von der Musik vielleicht ausgeht*].

Music is described as if it contained a kind of threat, as if it were capable of irremediably disconcerting the precious capacity this belabored people has for making do. And the narrator isolates this capacity in the careful syntax of an isolated clause, in the enclave of two dashes that edge and delimit the exception: "—only it has not happened—."

Josephine, then, this Josephine who is said to be "ours" (*unsere*), is this absolute exception (*Ausnahme*). She is the isolated clause, this unique *case* that gestures toward a form of bliss that the narrative's "we" does not even desire. Perhaps does anything but desire. A musical happiness that is perhaps not far from promising the worst of catastrophes to which this "we" remains absolutely foreign, even if, as what follows suggests, it is indeed in the presence of Josephine that this "we" seems most properly to gather together. As if Josephine gave voice to a promise that, *precisely because it does not concern us*, constitutes us as a "we" that is all the more urgent.

At any rate, by a retroactive effect of reading, the first sentence's possessive trembles: How can "our singer" be ours, how can she belong to "us," we who have in common only the fact of having nothing in common with her?

But the name that identifies Josephine also trembles: "singer" (*Sängerin*).

For it would appear that Josephine does not actually *sing*. She only whistles, like any of the most ordinary mice do. In other words, what seems to be exceptional about her, what makes her the incarnation of a promise of happiness that interests no one because it is too far removed from daily concerns, is precisely what is most *common* about her. She seems to distinguish herself from this *us*—a "we" she gathers together around her very distinction—in and through a capacity that is beyond banal: It is *indistinct*.

When the narrator wonders why Josephine exerts such a fascination, he considers a first hypothesis: Her "singing (*Gesang*) is so great that even the most insensitive cannot be deaf to it." According to this hypothesis, her singing would therefore be capable of moving even this "we" that can say that "we are absolutely unmusical" (*wir sind doch ganz unmusikalisch*) (360, translation modified). But, the narrator continues, this hypothesis would imply that this singing was "extraordinary" (*ausserordentlich*) and even unheard-of:

> . . . that from her throat something is sounding which we have never heard before and which we are not even capable of hearing, something that Josephine alone and no one else can enable us to hear.

This is not the case, he says. Josephine's singing has absolutely nothing exceptional or unique about it, and apparently the mice know it and freely say so to one another, even if they do so discreetly.

> Among intimates [*im vertrauten Kreise*, in the circle of intimates] we admit freely to one another that Josephine's singing, as singing [*als Gesang*], is nothing out of the ordinary.

Of course, and this is not without its importance, this is not the same "we" who admit the ordinary, banal character of this singing: It is a smaller, more restricted "we," probably closer to a you and me than to the community of an audience (the German speaks of the admission made "to one another," *einander*, something that implies a regime distinct from the collective gathering). In short, through a certain kind of admission, this "we" breaks a part of Josephine's fascination or enchanting charm. This "we" is therefore a kind of "us within us," both included within (because they are mice among other mice) and nonetheless subtracted from its encompassing effect. It is a "we" that is perhaps not secret, but is at least intimate (*vertraut*).

But the question concerning Josephine's art remains: "Is it in fact singing at all?" (*ist es denn überhaupt Gesang?*), asks the narrator.

His impression, which he conveys by enveloping it with a certain caution, as if it were a hypothesis that he does not immediately endorse, is as follows: "Josephine does not sing but only pipes," as all the other mice commonly do. And "perhaps," he adds, she "hardly rises above the level of our usual piping," common to mice in general. This is then a piping that no one would dream of pretending "is an art" (*als Kunst auszugeben*) and that all pipe "without noticing it."

Thus, our singer no longer sings, has probably never sung, and she is only "ours" (she only constitutes us as an *us*) through the absolute exception situated in her very indistinction.

Here, we find a paradox, that of *exceptional banality*. It is one that Kafka masterfully deploys and that we will have to continue to read with great patience. For this is the very paradox of what we call "hits."

Just as when I listen to hits, those songs that are all so *exceptionally banal*, I am unable to avoid what the narrator of "Josephine" calls "the enigma . . . of the enormous effect she produces" (361, translation modified); she is that singer who sings no more than what everyone could hum to oneself. It is indeed an enormous effect, and one can hardly find an explanation for it, so much does it derive its force from what is most ordinary, sometimes even in the absence of singing or of voice.

Kafka's short story, into which I am tempted to read an allegory of the hits that populate our musical landscape, therefore hardly allows me to understand the effect itself, which it leaves as a mystery. What it does perhaps indicate, though, is something about those who, like us, are entirely shaken up and profoundly disturbed by the inexplicable effectiveness of banality as such. It may say something about our times and about our relation to time.

Us?

Who is this *we* that the triviality of Josephine's singing carries away beyond all resistance? And who is it that, in the short story, says *we*?

It is first and foremost the narrator who, rather than incarnating the voice of the people of mice subjugated by this singing without song, would rather be something like the somewhat detached historian of a *we* that resists history. At least this is how he presents himself once he ends up recognizing that danger contributes to Josephine's authority.

> True, she does not save us and she gives us no strength; it is easy . . . to stage oneself after the event as the savior of our people, who have always somehow managed to save themselves, although at the cost of sacrifices which make historians—generally speaking we ignore historical research entirely—quite horror-struck. And yet it is true that just in emergencies we hearken better than at other times to Josephine's voice [*in Notlagen noch besser als sonnst auf Josefinens Stimme horchen*]. (366)

Josephine's singing, therefore, does not give strength; it does not save this people from anything, since, one way or another, they save themselves. The narrator is not far from suggesting here that it would even be the very distress of the people that confers a voice upon Josephine. Or rather that Josephine, on the one hand, with her singular whistle-song, and the people, on the other hand, with its common whistling, would perhaps not yet be constituted entities already there and waiting to be confronted. In fact, there is perhaps not a people that exists before Josephine any more than there is a Josephine before the people and its dangers.

> This piping, which rises up where everyone else is pledged to silence, comes almost like a message from the whole people to each individual [*dieses Pfeifen, das sich*

> *erhebt, wo allen anderen Schweigen auferlegt ist, kommt fast wie eine Botschaft des Volkes zu dem einzelnen*]; Josephine's thin piping amid grave decisions is almost like our people's precarious existence [*armselige Existenz unseres Volkes*] amid the tumult of a hostile world. (367)

Is it then the case that the people holds itself together, "thinly," only thanks to this whistling, thanks, that is, to this "nothing concerning the voice" (*dieses Nichts an Stimme*) that, according to the narrator, Josephine is?

In that case, how old is this people, our people? What is its era, and what moments does it have? At what speed does something happen to it? What is the time of its events, of the remarkable facts that run their course through its history, this people that completely neglects historical research?

If we believe the narrator, this people would be both like children (who, as we like to think, have no memories yet) and like old men (who, as we like to think, have only too many).

"A kind of unexpended, ineradicable childishness pervades our people," says the narrator. And he adds: "From this childishness [*Kindlichkeit*] of our people Josephine too has profited since the beginning" (369). We are naive; we let ourselves be taken in by Josephine; we try to resist her, but she is craftier than we are. In front of her we are overgrown children. And yet we are also, as the narrator further says, "prematurely old" (*vorzeitig alt*).

> A certain weariness and hopelessness spreading from that leaves a broad trail [*mit breiter Spur*] through our people's nature, tough and strong in hope that it is in general. Our lack of musical gifts [*Unmusikalität*] has surely

> some connection with this; we are too old for music [*wir sind zu alt für Musik*]; its excitement [*Erregung*], its rapture [*Aufschwung*] do not suit our heaviness [*Schwere*]; wearily we wave it away. (369)

Still very young yet also already very old, both late and early: This temporal distension that pulls and stretches us forward and backward, this chronic oscillation between ages is our constitutive amusia, out of which music can nonetheless find its moment and its time, a time for which it is perhaps never time. At the same time, this is the time that allows us to become *us*, one sole people, united around a nothing of voice.

> Here in the brief intervals between their struggles our people dream [*traümt das Volk*]; it is as if the limbs of each were loosened [*es ist, als lösten sich dem Einzelnen die Glieder*], as if the harried individual once in a while could relax and stretch himself at ease in the great, warm bed of the community [*als dürfte sich der Ruhelose einmal nach seiner Lust im grossen warmen Bett des Volkes dehnen und stricken*]. And into these dreams, Josephine's piping drops note by note; she calls it pearl-like, we call it staccato; but at any rate here it is in its right place, as nowhere else [*an seinem Platze, wie nirgends sonst*], finding the moment wait for it as music scarcely ever does [*wie Musik kaum jemals den auf sie wartenden Augenblick findet*]. Something of our poor brief childhood is in it, something of lost happiness that can never be found again, but also something of active daily life, of its small gaieties, unaccountable and yet springing up and not to be obliterated. And indeed this is all expressed not in full round tones but softly, in whispers, confidentially, sometimes a little

> hoarsely [*manchmal ein wenig heiser*]. . . . We certainly should not want to do without these performances. (370)

At these moments when, in a way, we are waiting for ourselves, music *happens*. And what is properly incredible, strange, and inexplicable is the fact that, as the narrator puts it so eloquently, music itself seems to find and invent the moment, or the momentousness, that was waiting for it.

Who waits for whom in the luck of these moments when we no longer have an age, when we are both old and young? Who waits for whom in this instantaneous counterpoint where so many unheard-of syncopations seem to be both condensed and canceled out? Who joins whom in this temporal embrace, in this strette?

With Josephine's singing (very similar in many ways to the Gregorian chant of Gregor's squeaking in *The Metamorphosis*), everything comes together in such a way that it is as if time itself were crystallizing: This time that would be ours, a time in which, as the narrator puts it, the "lost happiness" of childhood seems, *in spite of it all* and in an *incomprehensible* way, capable of combining with "active life" and its ever so few and poor "small gaieties."

Josephine's singing without singing, her piping, would be something like the anthem of this people and of its time. Piping, or the gesture of whistling, actually connotes both the authority of the call (one whistles to call someone closer or to control a crowd) and the fragility of the ephemeral (one whistles to indicate a sudden and unexpected disappearance). This is so much the case that what sounds out in Josephine's singing seems related both to a work song[3] and to an idle distraction: In the refrain of this voice without voice one finds both the very slight gaiety of the belabored mice who get up early and their moments of leisure when the distress of their miserable existence appears to them.

The Josephinian *descant* (*déchant*) would therefore be the national anthem that brings this people together. It would be its *voice*, but in the form of a "nothing of voice." And of an anthem to nothing.

CHAPTER 9 Musicology and Melology: Prince, Eros, and Copyright

Kafka and his *Josephine* whispered a sort of open secret into our ears: The hit speaks of nothing other than itself. In other words it speaks about nothing, quite literally, since it is an *anthem to nothing.*[1]

Yet let us not forget that this was already what that ur-hit "Parole, parole, parole" was saying in its own way, whether sung by Mina and Alberto Lupo or by Dalida and Alain Delon in the French cover of it. Listening to the words ("words, words, nothing but words") exchanged between the Spoken and the Sung, the hit did indeed appear to be something like the opening of a space *between* the song and itself, *between* its words and its song. As if in order to produce itself, the hit really produced a *discourse* about itself. We might call this a *musicology of the hit.* As if the hit, a subject, were speaking as a musicologist of itself, about the object it is for itself as it is produced between words and music, between the *logos* of discourse and the *melos* of song.

A melology in sum: a dialogue between self and self in the form of a melologue[2] that we could also find, though in less pure forms than in "Parole, parole, parole" in many successful hits.

For example, when Claude François sings "Magnolias Forever" in 1977, the hit, of course, appears to recount an ill-fated love story and a breakup. "I can't do anything about it anymore" (*Je ne peux plus rien y faire*), he cries, while the chorus, in English, comments: "Your girl is crying in the night." And the listeners we are cannot help but think: Yes, of course, he "doesn't know what to do" to console that poor girl he left, who is sobbing in the night. Yet almost immediately, almost without our noticing it and in a manner that is both obvious and discreet, the song starts talking about itself. It sings, "Tell her I am like her and that I always like the songs" (*Dites-lui que je suis comme elle, que j'aime toujours les chansons*); "tell her that I'm thinking of her when people talk to me about magnolias, when I hear these new pieces of music" (*dites-lui que je pense à elle, quand on me parle de magnolias, quand j'entends ces musiques nouvelles*). The title, "Magnolias," thus becomes a metonym for the songs one loves, faced with which one "no longer knows what to do," the songs one cannot resist. And at that point, the "you" of the song ("You look like her" [*Tu lui ressembles*], "and in your voice I sometimes hear some of her voice" [*et dans ta voix, j'entends parfois un peu sa voix*]) seems to be the song itself folded into a commentary on itself, enfolding the apparent object of his discourse ("your girl," that girl who cries into the night) over onto the subject she is when she stages herself as producing herself right under our eyes.

For the hit, as if it were apparently obsessed with itself even as it obsesses us, essentially sings its own becoming and its own time, a time that includes and envelops us in advance. In the 1971 hit "Le temps de ma chanson," Michel Fugain explicitly declares as much.

> During the time, in the time of my song /The water just flows and flows under the bridges of the world, /Some men are born and then others are gone/in the time of my song, in the time of my song.[3]

Once the preposition "in" has taken over for the word "during," time starts to take up space and becomes as hospitable as the world. And this same time, this same little bit of time that is nonetheless immense because it seeks to include within itself everything that happens, gives life to so many other hits on their globalized stage. To limit myself to the examples of my own personal top fifty, when Barry White sings "Let the Music Play," and he pretends to make music a metaphor for the night he is getting ready to spend with "her" (she who is at home), is he not actually speaking about his hit itself? "Let the music play on, keep the music strong, let it play on, let it play on, let it play on," he tirelessly repeats, as if he were ensuring himself, at the very moment he sings his song, that that song will be strong, that it will always reproduce itself, over and over, on and on.

This automusicology of comments on the hit under way from within the hit itself can be found in pretty much any hit: The hit declares its production of itself, its repetition always yet to come, thus opening and giving space to the *between* into which a refrain will rush. This melology is where the hit takes off, according to yet another allegory of itself, as it is sung in a beautiful version of Francesco De Gregori's song "La donna cannone" ["The Lady Cannonball"] (1983) by Ornella Vanoni.

> Applause from a paying audience will let you know/And from the mouth of the cannon, a song will resound/and

> with my hands, my love, with my hands I will take you/ And without saying a word in my heart, I will carry you.[4]

Here, too, at the threshold of the refrain that immediately follows these words, the hit addresses itself ("my love"), it carries itself away ("I will carry you") before taking off, like a cannon shot to launch the refrain, igniting the lyrical flight that produces the song within the song, on the stage that it has prepared for itself.

In the hit's musicology, it would thus certainly seem that we are touching on the heart of the hit ("I will carry you in my heart"). The heart: where, barely after having shot the cannon fire that echoes within its interior, the song takes its lyrics by the hand to take them, hand in hand, to the heart of itself as its refrain begins to rise.

Here we are at the heart of the hit: yes, the place where, while working toward itself, it pretends to think about another, about a "you," only the better to return to itself and produce . . . *itself.* As in the hit by Lucio Battisti, *E penso a te*, where the "you" the "I" is thinking of is most likely, yet again, the song itself.

> I am working—I think of you/Then I come home—I think of you/I call him and for a moment I think of you [*Io lavoro e penso a te/Torno a casa e penso a te/Le telefono e intanto penso a te*].

In short, the "I" of a hit thinks about itself. It thinks itself; it comments on itself; it produces itself as a musicologist of itself before anyone (whether I or another) can think about analyzing its production.

* * *

In the midst of the auto-musicological concert or festival brought to us by hits, Prince can be credited with having slipped in a supplementary turn or fold. With "Musicology," the title song of his eponymous album of 2004, Prince effectively redoubles the theatricality that, in songs such as "Parole, parole, parole," had already dug out a stage between the song and itself.

In this new theater, the décor has changed. The stage—as can also be seen in the video that now accompanies any hit—is a Harlem club where a party is taking place. On this stage, the song begins by evoking the technological, socio-historical, and musicological context for its own production. "Take your pick—turntable or a band?" asks the fourth couplet, while the preceding and following lyrics sketch out a list and a litany of names of artists from rap, hip-hop, funk, and soul who have made the recent or ancient history of pop: Doug E., who appeared several times on stage with Prince, is, according to the beginning of the song, invited to the party. Later on, the song names the rapper Chuck D. from Public Enemy, the group Earth, Wind and Fire with their 1978 and 1980 hits "September" and "Let's Groove," as well as the famous *Hot Pants*, an album by "James" (Brown) from 1971, and the 1969 hit by "Sly" (and the Family Stone), "I Want to Take You Higher."

Here, we certainly find the elements for a musicology within the hit, a kind of history of music *within* the song itself, compounded with allusions to the technical devices that condition it. (These last are particularly visible in the video, which emphasizes its shots of old used records at a record store.)

Prince is of course not the first to have done this: Let it suffice to mention Claude Nougaro, who, in the 1973 "Dansez sur moi" [Dance to me], sang phonography as an anthumous tombstone;[5] or else Laurent Voulzy's unforgettable 1977 "Rock Collection," which claimed to be a hit about hits, almost a history of rock in songs.[6] But what changes in the décor Prince has orchestrated as a space for the hit's self-production is that the stage has become a *theater of operations*, almost in the military sense of the term. The war waged here under the code name "funk soldiers" is a struggle for legitimacy that inscribes and engraves the hit into a history or a phonographic archive that is above all a battleground for musical merchandise.

When Prince speaks as an "I" in "Musicology," he takes the stage as a piece of merchandise. He speaks *as* a commodity, in its name and in the first person. And he knows this, and says so, explicitly, in an interview to which we will have to pay close attention.

"Joy in Repetition" is one of Prince's often forgotten songs, but it's a good one, even if it is buried in the insipid 1990 album *Graffiti Bridge*.

Before returning to "Musicology" and its melology of musical commodities that we have begun to analyze, it is worth our while to stick around a bit in this "club on 136th" that serves as a backdrop to the quick, banal and nonetheless exceptional love story lived out by the young man staged by Prince. In this club where "Joy in Repetition" is sung, one meets "poets" and "part-time singers," while a "band" plays a strange song. This song, as the song tells us, "is a year long." And when the young man "walked into the place," the song "had been playing for months." The song has been playing already for months now; it is there still being played. And yet, even though it has lasted so long, "no one seemed to care": A kind of general indifference reigns over the place, "an introverted 'this is it,' look on most of their faces."

At this point, and even though the young man is a regular at the club, for the first time ever he notices this woman "up at the mic repeating two words over and over again . . . this woman he had never noticed before." He loses himself "in the articulated manner in which she said them." Two words, just two words that must have been repeated so many times, two words for which the song, even while describing them and the way they are sung, keeps us waiting.

"These two words" are "Love me." Banal words of eros that have already been encountered in countless love songs stuck on repeat for years and years. But the song, this particular song, defers them, reserving the repetition of these words for its end, its end without end in a repetitive cyclone accompanied by the jubilation of the solo guitar. At this point of the song, it announces only the words, "these two words," separating them with its diction and with the rhythm of the three syllables (*these—two—words*) that describe them in an anticipated way: It's a triplet of syllables syncopated in relation to the general pulse of the song, as Prince's voice emphasizes, lasciviously, "a little behind the beat . . . just enough to turn you on." This is so much the case that what seems to ignite eros's desire is this gap, which, in advance, before the two banal words have even been uttered in the song, digs out time, the time for their repetition yet to come. Ultimately, the young man "could take no more" and ends up seizing "this woman" to drag "her from the stage . . . through the back door."

But who has the young man seized and taken away like this? He himself would like to know: "He said, 'Tell me, what's your name?'" She answers by repeating "the words again." So he won't actually know who she is, "this woman" whose voice is actually never heard, since it is only mentioned and transmitted through Prince's story. The one he seizes and drags off stage is actually perhaps not even a "who," a "someone," but repetition itself. The repetition that sets the song in motion, the repetition she pursues and which separates her from herself in that gap that is noted several times: "behind the beat," said Prince's voice when it commented on the diction of the two words. And he also describes it beautifully when he says that they were "two words falling between the drops." Between: in the gap dug out into the very heart of repetition.

From "Un air comme ça" to "Parole, parole, parole" and beyond, we have repeatedly verified an aspect of this hitological series that is now coming to a close: In the phantasmagoria of the hit, it is the musical commodity itself that speaks and sings, celebrating and commenting on its self-production as it repeats itself ad infinitum. The commodity itself draws us into the gap of its desire for itself, a desire that is always renewed since it is always deferred.

Prince, perhaps in spite of himself, understood and expressed this better than anyone when he told the story of where his name came from: Prince, a nickname for a sovereign in the globalized world of the market of major labels in the music industry. Or, more precisely, how the name came back to him from its dispossession, how it was repeated and reaffirmed like the hit itself.

In 1994, during the divisive negotiations with Warner Bros., his record company, for the release of the album *The Gold Experience*, Prince decided to have himself called an unpronounceable symbol ("the love symbol") that he used as a title for a 1992 album. He would appear in public with the word "slave" inscribed in capital letters on his cheek. And he declared:

> The first step I have taken towards the ultimate goal of emancipation from the chains that bind me to Warner Bros. was to change my name from Prince to the Love Symbol. Prince is the name that my mother gave me at birth. Warner Bros. took the name, trademarked it, and used it as the main marketing tool to promote all of the music that I wrote. The company owns the name Prince and all related music marketed under Prince. I became merely a pawn used to produce more money for Warner Bros. . . . I was born Prince and did not want to adopt another conventional name. The only acceptable replacement for my name, and my identity, was . . . a symbol with no pronunciation, that is a representation of me and what my music is about. This symbol is present in my work over the years; it is a concept that has evolved from my frustration; it is who I am. It is my name.[7]

Freed from his contract with Warner in 1999, Prince took up his own name again in 2000. However one judges the arguments for this reappropriation,[8] this episode of the unpronounceable symbol will have turned Prince into a kind of logo that comes close to looking like the copyright sign itself (©).

One can therefore understand that in the theater of operations of the album *Musicology*, the hit has become a product of economic and strategic war, as the musical commodity fights for its very soul, for the soul of its "musical self." And, taking up one of Benjamin's observations about Baudelaire's prose poems, one could say of Prince that "the commodity itself is the speaker here."[9]

This is in fact why the stage in *Musicology* for the self-production of the hit is turned around or upside-down, as if the sovereign musical commodity wanted to have the last word: It is no longer a scene of love, as it is in "Parole, parole, parole" or "Joy in Repetition," but a battle scene that takes place *at the end*, once the song has concluded with a kick in the direction of the "old school" ("Kick the old school joint/4 the true funk soldiers"). It is therefore no longer a question of staging the hit's desire in the hit, the desire that sets it into motion. Rather, it is a kind of coda that brands musical property in an echo of words that read like a legal injunction: "Don't you ever touch my stereo," we hear after other claims of similar ilk: "These are *my* records."

So at the close of his song, to enclose it onto itself at a stabilized market value, Prince enumerates samples of his past successes as so many copyrighted brands of himself: in chronological order, "If I Was Your Girlfriend," "17 Days," "Kiss," "Sign o' the Times," and "Little Red Corvette."

With this kind of legal registration of itself, which replaces Boris Vian's eternal love story between a "girl" and a "guy," the mercantile phantasmagoria that made for the great era of hits may be coming to a close. And our accounts of them as well, which, episode after episode, have tried to lend an ear to the way hits speak of themselves—that is, of the self-desiring machines that they are—by speaking about everything and nothing, about this and that.

CHAPTER 10 *This Is It: The King of Pop*

This is it: That's right, yes, this is really it; it's the Thing itself.[1]

It is happening here and now; it is coming; it announces itself. Here I am, it says and proclaims in speaking about itself. Here I am like the Thing in person, like the effective Thing, effectively.

"This is it," sings Michael Jackson in his last song, which is also the first of a long series of posthumous titles no doubt yet to come. We first hear the King of Pop's voice[2] asking if everyone is "ready," before it then counts to four, "one two three four." Then the piano starts: "This is it, here I stand . . ."

This is it. Here he is. The King of Pop.

This is it. There it is. The Thing.

Ecce homo. Ecce res.

The Thing, then, is the song that has just started up by saying "this is it," this is the song that it is. But this, the event of the Thing, is also immediately the erection of someone, of a sovereign "I" who is standing up ("Here I stand") in front of our very eyes. And we are immediately dazzled and blink our eyes, bathing in the suddenly blazing clarity. We squint our eyes through the halo of a blinding aura in an attempt to see who or what, *homo* or *res*, is rising to expand to the point of blending in to an infinite love: "I am the light of the world," he or it announces. "I feel grand," says the King, and this greatness and glory that I feel is love: "It is love I can feel."

Michael Jackson would, of course, have been the first one to protest in advance against the idea that is starting to be clear: In a February 1993 televised interview with Oprah Winfrey, he first confided that he loved to help children and that he "tr[ies] to imitate Jesus" before immediately reassuring Winfrey and the innumerable audience members: "I am not saying that I am Jesus, I'm not saying that." And in a December 22, 1993, televised declaration right in the middle of his first trial for pedophilia, he referred in a very uncomfortable way to Jesus's words from the Gospel of Luke, "Let the children come to me," before making it clear that "in no way do I think that I am God, but I do try to be God-like in my heart."

That these may be forms of denial is actually not all that important. What should give us pause is not what Michael Jackson himself may have thought or wanted to say, sincerely or not. What should give us pause is rather what will have been inscribed in and as a great musical, visual, and multimedia text. We lend an ear to a fable named Michael, as his fans would call him, and not to Michael Jackson himself. Down to certain of its kitschiest and most pop aspects, we auscultate a Christological figure whose death, it is said, garnered more internet comments than did John Paul II's.[3]

Michael J, then. As in Jesus.

Yet such a Christology, yes, this is it, an exemplary pop passion like his will have also been a planetary anthem—one hidden even as it was spread out in front of our very eyes—to another religion: the religion of capital and its globalized cult.

Before accepting a special prize as "Artist of a Generation" at the 1996 Brit Awards, Michael performed his "Earth Song" from the album *HIStory* that had come out the year before. At the back of the stage, the audience could see the Earth slowly rotating while Michael's silhouette began to appear with our blue planet as a background. Little by little and to the rhythm of gospel-inflected neo-evangelical music, children, as if called up by the apocalyptic ecological word transmitted by the lyrics that mention "the crying Earth," innumerable children, some of them carried in outstretched arms, emerged from the globe to gather around the singer surrounded by smoke and wind-machines. At the end, Michael shed his dark clothes to appear entirely dressed in white, an immaculate purity that drew the hands of all the innocent gathered by his side. All of them touch him, embrace him, and hold him tight. In a voice broken with emotion, Michael recalled the suffering in this world and all the children who die every minute of hunger, concluding with a message of hope and love: "I love you all; I believe in all of you; I love you."

Even more striking in its faith in a universal pop miracle, the 1995 video for this song of the Earth showed Michael stretched out, and almost crucified, between two calcified trees. His word alone, whether sung or cried out, was enough to entail the resurrection of animals being hunted and wounded, men being killed, and trees being cut down. With wide eyes, one watched the redemption of a destroyed world that needed care and healing, as the song "Heal the World" was already suggesting in 1991 with its video also calling thousands of children together, with candles, so that they might listen to the Michaelean gospel: "My brothers," he told them, "we have to heal the world with our love; love is strong."

So many other Christ-like moments could be unearthed in Michael's fable. The images for "Billie Jean," for example (directed by Steven Barron in 1983), show the star literally illuminating everything he touches: His footsteps on the sidewalk of a poor neighborhood transform each block of stone into a square of light; and the poor bum asleep next to a trashcan suddenly wakes up to the discovery that, after the angel passes, he is dressed in immaculate white. Michael is giving: Into the poor man's cup, he throws a coin that brings light.

What is the universal charity at work here? Is it the same one that pushed Michael to collaborate with Lionel Richie to write the song "We Are the World" in 1985?

This universal charity modeled on Christian or Christ-like love is, as "This Is It" literally says, the charity of indifference. Yes, that's it; that's just what the refrain of his posthumous song sings: "I never heard a single word about you, and I feel as though I've known you since a thousand years." This is it: This Thing that says "I" accomplishes the miracle of addressing itself to a "You" about whom it confesses it knows nothing but to whom it is indeed "destined." "I never thought that I would be your lover," but this is the way it is; "this is it"; the weak force, the passive passion of this charity that "I" am is stronger than everything else, and we can only submit and acquiesce to it.

Michael, the Thing named Michael, would therefore be a kind of infinite plasticity capable of espousing the form of each one of us, of changing and exchanging itself ad infinitum, like a universal currency, taking each of our most singular characteristics upon itself, taking them on in exchange, just as he takes the woes of the world upon himself. "It don't matter if you're black or white," as he sang on the 1991 album *Dangerous.* And in the gripping finale of the video for this hit directed by John Landis, Michael seemed to lend himself in advance to endless transformations in a kind of absolute passivity that sometimes made him a man and at others made him a woman, sometimes Chinese or Japanese and at others an American WASP, sometimes red-haired and others Rasta: in short, a chameleon face taking on all the characteristics of all races, nations, and classes in this world. In this scene that contributed to the popularization of morphing, Michael, through the plastic surgery of digital imagery, charitably lends himself to incessant deformation in favor of a humanity whose diversity is only apparent: In the one who effaces himself for the good cause, humanity is united, and it dances and gestures like one single man.

In Michael, in this Thing that he was and continues to be, charity is exchange. It's the indifference of general exchange—all equal and all equivalent—that concerns us all, each one of us in particular. In Michael and with Michael, what comes to fruition and accelerates is the *sanding* of humanity announced by Nietzsche in a posthumous fragment from 1880.

> The more the feeling of their unity with their fellow humans wins out over men, the more uniform they will become, the more rigorously they will feel any difference as immoral. Humanity's sanding thus necessarily appears: all the same, very small, very round. . . . Up until now, Christianity and democracy have brought humanity furthest onto the path of this metamorphosis into sand.

There were, of course, more than a few who got fed up with this, like the British singer Jarvis Cocker, who attempted to take the stage in protest during the intolerable Christological spectacle at the Brit Awards. This was of course pointless. Not only because of the security staff and bodyguards blocking all access to this charitable corpus that designated itself as such—"this is it"; *hoc est corpus meum*; this is my body. But above all because by acting this way, one forgets that Michael's anthemic force and capacity to bring people together draws from a much deeper source, one that has its roots in a history that cannot be limited to the shiny, tacky surface of the society of the spectacle and show business.

Where does this force come from, then? What gives it its vigor?

The passive passion of charity, writes Paul in his first letter to the Corinthians (13:7), "believeth all things, hopeth all things, endureth all things." Such is the infinite love (*agapê* in Paul's Greek) that is the foundation in advance for everything that will happen, a love that lies beneath (*hupomenei*) everything that can happen. Charity is like that archangelic Michaelean face (Michael, you will remember, is the only one to be described as an archangel in the Bible), like that face that is the ground that carries or bears all faces and which, for this very reason, is capable of appearing everywhere, of showing through or flashing up at any moment: Michael's fans, as we learned last August, are therefore coming in crowds after his death to contemplate his reincarnated traits on an Egyptian bust dating from three thousand years ago and conserved at the Field Museum in Chicago;[4] but already in 2005, toast was being sold on eBay—yes, slices of toasted bread—whose grill-marks had miraculously inscribed Michael's effigy, I swear, like that of Christ inscribed on Veronica's veil.[5] This is it; *ecce homo*.

Yet as we have seen, the spectrogram of the archangelical face is also that of infinite interchangeability. As if the *morphing* of the Veronico-Michaelean face made it into a general equivalent for all human face-nesses, as if it were their currency, the precious and charitable face thus revealing its preciousness and its price.

Michael is, according to his becoming-effigy, therefore of course the *archangel of exchange*; but above all else, as we will see, this is what his songs sing, the songs that will have borne his message without message better than any image can.

"This is it" is exemplary in this regard. "This Is It," that's just it, says nothing, transmits no content other than its own event: Yes, this is it, this event, which is itself, as we will hear, nothing beyond the advent of exchange. "This is it" would in this sense, therefore, be the formula of Michael's posterity, the formula of his infinite resurrection and transubstantiation in an endless (ex)change.

Not only, to start with, because these words, "This is it," were everywhere during the March 5, 2009, press conference when Michael announced that his concerts in London would be his last ever: "This is it," he declared, while his fans chanted the same three words. "I just want to say these will be my final show performances in London." It was thus a scene, even a kind of Last Supper [*Cène*], more auto-testamentary than ever before, with Michael saying that "this will be it . . . this is it . . . and when I say this is it . . . it really means this is it."

Not only, second, because *This Is It* is the title of the posthumous film that will have brought Michael back to life on movie screens around the world in a postmortem tour as grandiose and spectrally triumphant as the ones he went on while he was alive.

But also, finally and most importantly, because "this is it" was the formula for the apparent self-evidence that accompanies the birth of songs, those Christo-Michaelean miracles. He had written as much in his 1988 autobiography called *Moonwalk*: "In the end, many songs kind of create themselves, you just say: this is it."[6]

It therefore seems obvious: Yes, this is it; here is the song; *ecce cantus*. But by announcing itself this way, this song is immediately exchanged with an "I": "Here I stand"; that's it; here is a "Me"; *ecce ego*; *ecce Michael*. And this "I" of the song gives itself to each of us with love; he gives himself to us all. If he is, as he sings, "the light of the world," if he feels so "grand," it's because he is filled in advance with infinite love; "it is love I can feel," a love for a You, anyone at all, all of us, his faithful someone this "I" feels it has known since the beginning of time: "And it feels as though I've seen your face a thousand times," he sings, and he makes us avow and confess in advance that we ourselves know him, "and you said you really know me yourself."

By acting this way, the song acts as a vast mechanism of exchange or conversion: It itself, this is it, becomes "I," "here I stand," and this "I" in turn becomes Michael's Christ-like light, the light of his love that has known us forever and that we have forever known, that lends itself to us as we lend ourselves to him.

Michael was already singing of the self-evidence of these exchanges of the Thing and within the Thing during the Jackson Five era. A song like "(You Were Made) Especially for Me," that figures on the 1995 retrospective album *Soulstation*, stated that each one of us, each listener, each faithful fan was indeed made to be so; in short, that we were and always will be, however many of us there are, especially and specifically made for this, yes, this is it, for this Thing that addresses itself to us by saying "I," "here I stand," and singing to us that it loves us, "you're definitely my kind of loving." I came across one of my favorite comments by a fan on youtube, about the interpretation of "(You Were Made) Especially for Me" during the Jacksons' Variety Show in 1977: "I was made especially for Mike," declares someone under the moniker because0011. And even if I will never know who because0011 is, he or she will have answered, in advance and on behalf of us all, to the *causality* induced by the song in its relation to itself: I was made, we answer each time, I was fabricated especially for Michael, for that Thing named Michael who can say "I" thanks to the obviousness of a "this is it" that accompanies the auto-presentation of the thingly Self inscribed within general interchangeability.

In 1987, "I Just Can't Stop Loving You," that incredibly famous single from the album *Bad* sung as a duet with Siedah Garrett, made the Christological dimension of the love the song bears *within itself* for the one to whom it is addressed even clearer. This time, the sung Thing, not content to say "I" as a way to address some "You," doubled itself into an I-You, thus itself becoming a scene of address to the other in oneself as a way of celebrating the celestial character of the exchange: "Our love is dawning," sang Michael, "heaven's glad you came," while another voice, the voice of the other in him, Siedah Garrett's, answered that she heard him, "I hear your voice now" and that "heaven's in my heart" when "I hear harps, and angels sing" to glorify this encounter.

This is how the Thing sung is *heard* and *understood*. This is its evidence; this is it, its way of coming into its own and of understanding *itself*; yes, this is it; this is its understanding of itself within itself. This is the auto-referentiality of the hit closed in on itself but doubled into two, this is its tautegorical closure onto itself, and this is what conditions, as I tried to show in earlier chapters, its infinite interchangeability, the limitless generosity and charity with which it lends itself to everything.

Let us now lend an ear to "Man in the Mirror," one of Michael's biggest hits, composed by Siedah Garrett for the album *Bad*: "I'm starting with me," sings this humanitarian song, of course as a way of preaching to each one of us that we need to change ourselves before we can consider changing the world, but also, beyond these declared good intentions, as if the hit confessed that to be exchanged, to divert attention from itself, it must first say itself; it must begin by instigating a relation to itself by becoming the mirror of itself. "I'm starting with the man in the mirror," the hit affirms, because the reflection by which each one of us is inscribed in advance in the narcissism of the Thing is what allows it to point to itself as the site par excellence of exchange.[7]

The complete paradigm of the exchangeable Thing is money.

And money has always had something sacred and sacrificial about it, in the manner of Eucharistic wafers, which, as Marc Shell has reminded us,[8] were the currency of Christ because they were struck and minted like coins and were said to represent the body of Jesus and be worth Him, while the wafers affirmed the faith in the very possibility of that exchange. Some even interpret the dollar sign ($) as a derivation of the inscription HIS, *in hoc signo*, the "by this sign" that figures on Christian Eucharistic wafers.[9]

Whatever the case may be, in order for it to be the object of exchange that it is, in order for it to incarnate exchange itself, money has to designate itself as such. It must always, in one way or another, bear the self-designating mark of the monetary sign it is.

In hoc signo, this is it.

Yes, that's it; a mark such as this participates in what Giorgio Agamben has described as the paradigm of an "economic theology"[10] whose sources he traces to Christian Patrology. Lacking the space to reconstitute Agamben's patient analyses, we might follow them to say that if the Trinity and the Incarnation of the Son participate in an *oikonomia*, and even in a "mystery of economy," the transubstantiation of the Eucharist pursues this original exchange. It converts its original vicariousness in what is called the Eucharistic species: the wine or the bread, the Eucharistic wafers. And when the Eucharistic wafer becomes a coin—a token, as was the case with *méreaux* in Calvin's time, coins of exchange that made participation in the Eucharist possible—it generally bears the sign of the sign that it is: *in hoc signo*.

These are no doubt the reasons why Walter Benjamin, in "Capitalism as Religion," a posthumous fragment from 1921 whose importance has yet to be fully appreciated, proposed a "comparison between the images of the saints of the various religions and the banknotes of different states" as a way of grasping "the spirit that speaks from the ornamental design" of paper money.[11] A spirit (*Geist*) that, although hidden, exists in the faith, in the confidence or credit implied in every act of exchange.

The glory of this *fiduciary* spirit may well be what Michael is singing. Not only on "Money," from the 1995 *HIStory* album, where his refrain hammers out, "Anything, anything, anything for money." But also and perhaps especially when, on "Keep the Faith" from the 1991 album *Dangerous*, he intones a hymn to sustained faith and fiduciary returns: "The power's in believing," he says, "so keep the faith, baby yeah; it's just a matter of time before your confidence will win out; go and keep it brother; just keep your eyes on the prize."

What we hear in between Michael's words here, between the lines of this anthem to faith sung by the archangel of exchange, is the good old proverb that tells us that "time is money." Benjamin Franklin recalled this proverb in his famous 1738 *Advice to a Young Tradesman*, that foundational document that Max Weber considered an illustration of the spirit of capitalism "in almost classical purity."[12] Franklin was telling his young friend: "Remember that time is money," and even "remember that credit is money." And finally, remember that money has a "prolific, generative nature," since "money can beget money . . . and its offspring can beget more, and so on."

For all the exorbitant auction prices of Michael's relics (at the November 21, 2009, auction in New York, for example, where his glove was sold for $350,000 and the black jacket from the *Bad* tour for $225,000), for all that his image has been appropriated by inestimable works of pop art (the most famous being Jeff Koons's *Michael Jackson and Bubbles*, a porcelain sculpture covered in gold and sold for six million dollars in 2001), it is of course the King of Pop's songs that will have realized the miracle whose secret Franklin claims to reveal: *The Way to Make Money Plenty*. . . . And if these songs will have generated profits never equaled in the history of the music industry, breaking all records of profitability, it is also because, before they enter into the market of the hit parade, they will have staged the infinite quest for profitable exchange in an auto-affirmation of themselves, in an auto-injunction to be converted and to multiply into innumerable copies of themselves.

"Keep the Faith" is a pure illustration of this: The faith that must be kept, the faith that opens access to any and all rewards and prizes, is the faith in the very imperative to "keep the faith." In other words, in the final analysis, which never arrives, it is the credit given to this anthem to exchange that the song singing it actually is. "Keep the faith" means "keep the faith"; yes, that's it; this is it; keep on and keep on repeating this very song, "Keep the faith"; let's have faith in it, in its fiduciary character, to engender with it, in us, and on the market its infinite and obsessive offspring.

Under the pretext of singing about the love of one person or another, there are many other songs by Archangel Michael that are actually singing their own credit. "I Just Can't Stop Loving You" is thus above all an address, a declaration of the song's love for itself, in the form of a circular doubling into I-You which makes the song say, *in and of itself*: "I just can't stop loving I just can't stop loving you." And so on and so forth, vertiginously so.

In the same way, on "I Can't Help It" from the mythic 1979 album *Off the Wall*, the song looks at itself in the mirror ("looking in my mirror") and pretends to be surprised ("took me by surprise"). It can't help seeing itself ("I can't help but see you"), loving itself in the narcissism of the Thing that starts to multiply ("I can't help but love you") and loving itself even more every time it repeats itself ("it's getting better all the time") in an irresistible auto-affection that leaves us with no chance whatsoever ("I can't help it"), that has already conquered us when it promises us a heavenly prize ("heaven is the prize.")

Yet it is "Don't Stop 'til You Get Enough," one of the biggest hits of all time since its 1979 release, that states in crystal-clear and irresistibly seductive terms the structure of the Michaelean hit, a structure both proliferating and closed into a loop (in the video for the song, Michael himself actually seems to multiply): In this case, the hit states its own "power," its strength, and its wish ("the force the vow"), what it is "that makes it happen" without knowing why or how ("it asks no questions why"), which simply means that the song, this very song, doesn't stop and will never stop ("don't stop, don't stop 'til you get enough.")

This is the naïveté and the powerful, narcissistic candor of the Michaelean hit. It is its *exchangelism*, the message borne by this angelic messenger: Its good news, its Gospel says nothing other than itself and its faith in itself. Within itself as a stage for the first change that will be infinitely pursued in exchange.

Keep the Faith, this is it, yes, that's it, don't stop, keep on, you were made especially for me.

In his 1921 fragment titled "Capitalism as Religion," Benjamin wrote:

> A religion may be discerned in capitalism—that is to say, capitalism serves essentially to allay the same anxieties, torments, and disturbances to which the so-called religions offered answers. The proof of the religious structure of capitalism, not merely, as [Max] Weber believes, as a formation conditioned by religion, but as an essentially religious phenomenon—would still lead even today to the folly of an endless universal polemic. We cannot draw closed the net in which we are caught.[13]

Nothing indicates that we can decipher this very short text, these dense pages, especially since they themselves begin by confessing a certain impossibility: "We cannot draw closed the net in which we are caught" (*das Netz in dem wir stehen zuziehen*). Nothing then can guarantee our ability to hear the tale of what holds us, what constitutes and ensnares us. And yet, I would like to turn to these pages as a way of concluding and in order to try to better hear Michael's fable, in order to lend an ear to what he announces, the news of his new New Testament.[14]

Benjamin's thinking was attentive, in a way no other thinking has been able to be, to kitsch, advertising, photography, movies and their stars, department stores—in short, to many of the elements of what we would today call "pop culture" without in fact knowing what exactly we mean by that term. Yet when, in this fragment, he interrogates the religious nature of capitalism, Benjamin's discourse is lapidary and enigmatic, to say the least. Without justifying or really arguing for them, he identifies and lists the "three aspects of this religious structure of capitalism" (in reality, there will be four).

First, writes Benjamin, "capitalism is a purely cultic religion," *eine reine Kultreligion*. In other words, in it there is nothing but a cult: "Capitalism has no specific body of dogma, no theology." And second, he adds, "The cult is permanent." Capitalism admits no "weekday," no *Wochentag*.

In reality, these first two characteristics are only one. If the capitalist cult is not the celebration of a dogma or a principle, if it is in the service of nothing at all, if it does not cultivate a message, this is because it has its value in and of itself as the cult of the cult it is. And in this sense it must be permanent; it must be practiced night and day, "Working Day and Night," as Michael sings it on the album

Off the Wall. This cult that refers only to itself,[15] a cult immanent to itself, is henceforth the celebration of the mystery of the "this is it." That's it, yes, what we are celebrating in capitalism is nothing other than what we celebrate, this is it, that's it, "and when I say this is it, it really means this is it."

A cult of cult, then, which cannot stop *celebrating itself*, over and over, always more, don't stop, keep the faith, don't stop 'til you get enough.

Benjamin, however, seems to indicate an end and a term to this cult. An end without end or a term without term, which gives him his third characteristic: The capitalist cult of the capitalist cult, in its permanent auto-celebration, would aim for the universalization of what Benjamin, in German, calls *Schuld.* It is difficult to translate with only one word a word that, in German, indissociably means both guilt and debt, in an economic sense.

> And third, the cult makes debt pervasive [*ist verschuldend*]. Capitalism is probably the first instance of a cult that creates debt, not atonement. . . . A vast sense of debt [*ein ungeheures Schuldbewusstsein*] that is unable to find relief seizes on the cult, not to atone for this debt [*Schuld*] but to make it universal . . . so as once and for all to include God in the system of debt. . . . The nature of the religious movement which is capitalism entails endurance right to the end, to the point where God, too, finally takes on the entire burden of debt [*die endliche völlige Verschuldung Gottes*].[16]

The god whose cult is celebrated in capitalism is, therefore, in the last analysis, indebtedness itself. Completely indebted, God becomes the Debt—and vice versa. As for Michael, he may not quite have been this God-Debt, but he will have been the archangel of exchange, a multimillionaire racking up profits like no one else while accumulating an abyssal debt, which seemed to grow at the same rate as his wealth.[17] Between the trials where he stood accused and his measureless indebtedness, the two valences of Benjamin's *Schuld* are inextricable in Michael's pop passion, where he is both guilty and indebted.

What we therefore need to hear in Benjamin's enigmatic fragment is that the end of the capitalist cult to the capitalist cult is the *becoming-debt* of divinity itself. The horizon or target of this cult, which is only the cult of nothing other than itself, would therefore be the pure deferred and fiduciary structure of infinite credit and infinite debt.

This is why, as Benjamin adds a fourth characteristic to the three he had announced, the god of this cult "must be hidden," kept secret (*verheimlicht*). One must not know, one must not be able to address a god who has become debt, entirely indebted. One must not be able to address him, to worship him as such, as debt. For a Debt-God would never be able to be stabilized and posed as such—he can only be deferred until later, indefinitely, and can only be a debtor in his own eyes. He needs, like the King of Pop, other faces, infinitely many other faces.

We will therefore never know whether or not Michael may have been the Christic incarnation of such a god. At best, we can consider that he will have been its archangel, angel, or some kind of celestial minister for it.

What is certain is that we owe him a lot.

Our debt is infinite, as was his—a *capital* debt.

When Oprah Winfrey asked him an embarrassing question in a 1993 television interview, Michael answered: "Ask the music."

That is what we have done.

And it answered back: Keep the faith, don't stop, this is it.

NOTES

Preface: Especially for the English-language Reader

1. Theodor W. Adorno, "Commodity Music Analysed," in *Quasi una fantasia: Essays on Modern Music*, trans. Rodney Livingstone (London: Verso, 1998), 45.
2. Edgar Allan Poe, "The Imp of the Perverse," in *Poetry and Tales* (New York: Library of America, 1984), 830–31.
3. Slavoj Žižek, *Living in the End Times* (London: Verso, 2011), 366–71.

1. Earworms: Life's Soundtrack

1. "Can't Get It Out of My Head," *Guardian,* June 22, 2006, http://www.guardian.co.uk/music/2006/jun/22/popandrock, accessed February 11, 2010. Thanks to my friend Hervé Aubron for drawing my attention to this article.
2. See www.business.uc.edu/earworms/vc.
3. "Wherever you go, iPod is ready to play the soundtrack of your life." This phrase could be read recently as an advertising slogan on a commercial website. Melomaniacs like myself have appropriated the expression, which is spreading in discussion forums.

2. The Banal and the Singular

1. "Elle fait donner sur le pavé/Un air comme ça/Dou da da dou dah/Dou da da dou daiah . . . —Il vint passer en sifflotant/Un

air comme ça/(sifflé . . .)—Ils se sont r'gardés très étonnés/ Elle a d'mandé:/'Comment ça s'fait-y que vous la sachiez,/J'suis épatée . . ."/—Il a répondu:/(parlé) "Ben, eu, je, j'la connais pas,"/(sung) "C'est venu comme ça . . ."/"Dou da da dou dah/ Dou da dou da dou dah, dou da, dou dah. . . ." (Translation mine.)

2. This fact was noted by Olivier Nuc and Jean-Pierre Nataf at a conference/concert organized by the Halle de la Chansons at the Maroquinerie (October 22, 2005). "It is Vian who invented the word 'tube.' . . . [W]hen he was artistic director [first with Philips in 1957 and later with Barclay], he replaced the then-current term 'saucisson' [sausage] with 'tube.' "
3. Boris Vian, *En avant la zizique . . . et par ici les gros sous, Pauvert/ Le Livre de poch* (Paris: Pauvert/Livre de Poche, 1997), 45–46: "The distribution of modern 'popular' music and its proliferation around the world has happened in such a way that one can establish well-defined principles; when pure and simple businessmen carefully apply these principles, they can sometimes replace inspiration. If one takes one's intuition of a fashion one senses, the demands of a singer at the height of his career who is able to predict what his public wants from him, the needs of an editor who is led by competition or resolute in gambling with songs like one gambles on the stock market, it is possible to create from nothing, totally cold or almost cold, a 'hit' [tube]—a song destined to 'be a big success.' " And on page 88: "There is a kind of editor whose ideal reference would produce hits [tubes] by the kilometer." (Translation mine.)
4. "V'là les accessoires pour faire un succès./Une rue, un trottoir, une même bien roulée./Un gars, chandail noire et cheveux collés./Rengaine qui traîne, ni triste ni gaie . . ./Voilà les accessoires, Messieurs dames, entrez!/La fille et le gars se sont rencontrés./ Entre eux deux, y a soudain quelque chose qui survient,/Dans la nuit les voilà partis." (Translation mine.)
5. "My story is a love story./My complaint is the complaint of two hearts./A novel like so many others/That might be yours./People from here or from elsewhere . . . —It's the story of a love, eternal and banal./My story is the story everyone knows./Those who

love one another play the same tune, this I know/But naive or profound,/It's the only song in the world/That will never end." (Translation mine.) (Thanks to Jean-Luc Nancy who, reminding me of this song, writes, "The story is reduced to the bare minimum of a love story where the 'This is the story' refers to the song itself—'This is . . .' not what is sung, but the fact of singing." We will get back to this point.)

6. "For some, beautiful love songs/are all alike./It's always the same production./Those jaded success stories don't want to betray/The fact that they know how to cry . . . —They are clichés designed to ensnare/All those who are alone and forgotten." (Translation mine.)
7. "But all the songs/Tell the same story,/There is always a boy/And a girl in despair . . ./A melody you hear everywhere." (1984, with Véronique Jannot—the lyrics are by Alain Souchon.) (Translation mine.)
8. Karl Marx, "The Fetishism of Commodities and the Secret Thereof," in *Capital: A Critique of Political Economy*, 1.4.18. Subsequent references to this work will be given by page number in parentheses in the text.
9. Cf. Walter Benjamin, "The Paris of the Second Empire in Baudelaire," trans. Harry Zohn, in *Walter Benjamin: Selected Writings*, vol. 4, ed. Howard Eiland and Michael W. Jennings (Cambridge, Mass.: Harvard University Press, 2003), 31. Benjamin even considers this "point of view" of the commodity as a possible self-reflection: "The commodity wants to look itself in the face" ("Central Park," ibid., 173).
10. Many notes in *The Arcades Project* mention this "intoxication of empathy felt by the flâneur," which Benjamin characterizes in the following way: "Empathy with the commodity is fundamentally empathy with exchange value itself. The flâneur is the virtuoso of this empathy. He takes the concept of marketability itself for a stroll." *The Arcades Project*, trans. Howard Eiland and Kevin McLaughlin, prepared on the basis of the German volume ed. Rolf Tiedemann (Cambridge, Mass.: Harvard University Press, 1999), 448.
11. Walter Benjamin, "Some Remarks on Folk Art," trans. Rodney Livingstone, in *Walter Benjamin: Selected Writings*, 2:278–79.

12. Ibid., 279, emphasis added.
13. Siegfried Kracauer, *Jacques Offenbach and the Paris of His Time,* trans. Gwenda David and Eric Mosbacher (New York: Zone, 2001), 44, translation modified.
14. *Allegory* comes from the Greek word *allos,* "other," and *agoreuiein,* "speaking (in public)." Thus saying something different from what is literally said. But, citing a phrase from Schelling who is himself borrowing it from Coleridge, it would perhaps be more precise to say that the song is tautegorical, that it says itself as another. This would bring it close to the myth, as Jean-Luc Nancy has described it in *The Inoperative Community* (ed. Peter Conner with a foreword by Christopher Fynsk [Minneapolis: University of Minnesota Press, 1991], 49): "[The myth] says nothing other than itself. . . . It does not need to be interpreted, since it explains itself. . . . [It is] the mythology that explains or interprets itself." Just like the hit, which is therefore also its own musicology—and no doubt its own mythology.
15. Several recent websites now propose this kind of "service": http://www.hitsongscience.com, for example. On the home page, one finds big letters that spell out the question, "Is your song a potential hit?" A word of welcome lists the criteria the online software will use to analyze the melodic samples submitted by the user.
16. Søren Kierkegaard, *Repetition,* trans. Howard V. Hong and Edna V. Hong (Princeton: Princeton University Press, 1983). Subsequent references to this work will be given by page number in parentheses in the text. For a fine reading of *Repetition* to which my reading is indebted, see Samuel Weber, "Kirkegaard's Posse," in *Theatricality as Medium* (New York: Fordham University Press, 2004). [*Translator's note:* The French translation of *Repetition* to which Szendy's reading refers is titled *La Reprise,* a word that is also used to name a "cover version" of a hit. This resonance is obviously lost in the English translation of Kierkegaard's title.]
17. In his letter to Constantius dated January 13, the young man excuses himself for "burden[ing] you with my everlasting refrain." Kierkegaard, *Repetition,* 213.

18. [*Translator's note:* The term references a "tube," the French word for a hit.]

19. Nor, for that matter, any more than money is, as Constantin says, introducing a monetary or economic analogy that we will pick up again a little later on in our discussion of hits. In a "little annex" to *Repetition* (that is collected in his *Papers* from 1843–44), Kierkegaard speaks ironically of the Hegelian system, "in the sense that every teller in our philosophical bank could count: 1–2–3 . . ." The irony of this bank accounting does indeed aim at Hegel and a "modern philosophy [that] makes no movement," except into immanence, and which contents itself with "mak [ing] only a commotion about sublation [*Ophaevelser,* Danish translation for the German *Aufhebung*]" (318, translation modified). To the bank of Hegelian dialectics (about which Marx, in the very same year in his *Manuscripts from 1844,* said that "logic is the money of spirit"), Kierkegaard implicitly opposes, as we will see, the "lottery" of repetition. Whose profits, as Job's example makes clear, are never certain. Whose revenues only return—if they do, if there is repetition—through the experience of an absolute blockage or clotting in the tubular canalizations of the system. In this sense, the category of repetition in Kierkegaard is not far from announcing the impossible event or the impossible decision whose paradoxical logic was underlined in the thinking of Jacques Derrida.

20. In French, *s'engouer* is first of all, in an antiquated usage, to choke by swallowing too quickly, to block one's *gosier* (gullet) by taking something in too avidly. Its etymology seems to derive the word from a pre-Latin origin that can also be found in *joue* (cheek) (in its old dialectical form of *goue*) and in the verb *gaver* (to stuff with food). In this sense, then, *engouement* is therefore an *engorgement* (obstruction). But *s'engouer,* in the supposedly figurative sense, is also of course to get wrapped up in something, to allow oneself to be taken by an excessive and most often ephemeral passion. [*Translator's note: Engouement* can thus be translated both, in a medical sense, as an obstruction and, in its figurative sense, as enthusiasm. Because both senses are important to Szendy's use of the term, we have chosen to translate it as "obstructive enthusiasm."]

3. The Filmography of Hits

1. [*Translator's note:* In both the title of this chapter ("*Le Cinéma des Tubes*") and in the phrase I have translated as "their own kind of production," Szendy's French refers to the French slang expression "faire son cinéma," which means to exaggerate or to be hysterical.]
2. Theodor Reik, *The Haunting Melody: Psychoanalytic Experiences in Life and Music* (New York: Grove Press, 1960). Subsequent references to this work will be given by page number in parentheses in the text.
3. This is more or less what Philippe Lacoue-Labarthe says in his beautiful reading of Reik's essay. See "The Echo of the Subject," in *Typographies*, trans. Christopher Fynsk (Stanford, Calif.: Stanford University Press, 1998), when he points out what he calls an "attempt . . . of *translation*, to reduce the acoustic (and the musical) to the verbal" (155).
4. I am citing comments by the screenplay writer and director gathered for the DVD edition of the film.
5. In *La Haine de la musique* (Paris: Calmann-Lévy, 1996, 60), Pascal Quignard speaks of a "*fredon resurgi*," or a "hum returned."
6. "Ce n'est rien . . . tu sais bien. . . . elles s'en vont comme les bateaux, et soudain, ça revient."
7. ". . . ça s'en va et ça revient, c'est fait de tout petits riens . . ."
8. ". . . cette impression de déjà-vu, d'être déjà passé par là; je suis sûr d'avoir entendu avant ce soir cette chanson-là . . ."
9. "Repetition and recollection," wrote the narrator of Kierkegaard's *Repetition*, "are one and the same movement, but in opposite directions" (131).
10. [*Translator's note:* Szendy uses the expression *par raccroc* to describe what I have translated as "lucky breaks." The French expression therefore resonates with *raccrocher*, or "to hang up the phone."]
11. "Il peut m'arriver n'importe quoi,/J'm'en fous pas mal./J'ai mon amant qui est à moi,/c'est peut-être banal."
12. "Il y a ses bras qui m'enlacent,/il y a son corps, doux et chaud."
13. Theodor Reik, "The Unknown Murderer," in *The Compulsion to Confess* (New York: Grove Press, 1961). Reik's essay notes many

musically marked clues, and they would gain from being studied one by one, from the victim's singing bone in a tale by the Grimms to Miss Odel's phonograph in S. S. Van Dine's *Canary Murder Case.*

14. Because Peter Lorre did not know how to whistle, it has been said that it is actually Fritz Lang's whistling that we hear on the soundtrack.
15. This is the "ambiguity" of the *ritournelle,* or refrain, that Deleuze and Guattari describe in *A Thousand Plateaus* (trans. Brian Massumi [London: Continuum, 2004], 359) as being "between the territory and deterritorialization."
16. Benjamin, *Arcades Project,* 420.
17. See in particular the letter from Adorno to Benjamin dated November 10, 1938, where he chastises Benjamin for "a deficiency . . . linked to the fact that the capitalist function of the ragpicker—to subject even begging to exchange value—is unarticulated" (Benjamin, *Selected Writings,* 4:103). In his essay on Baudelaire, Benjamin does nonetheless write, "When the new industrial processes gave refuse a certain value, ragpickers appeared in the cities in larger numbers" (ibid., 8).
18. Ibid., 166.
19. On espionage in general, and in Hitchcock in particular, see my *Sur écoute: Esthétique de l'espionnage* (Paris: Minuit, 2007).
20. Cf. Jacques Derrida, "Freud and the Scene of Writing," in *Writing and Difference,* trans. Alan Bass (Chicago: University of Chicago Press, 1978).
21. A very strange metonymic logic is at work here: After having been lost, like a detail or a part that could be replaced by another in the memory where it was inscribed, the tune comes back, but on a larger scale than its mnemonic container, since it has incorporated the function of its substitute or its rival (the wedding march) and is now amplified to the dimensions of a space that welcomes its own bearers (Gilbert, the vehicle for the clandestine melody hidden *within him,* now enters *into it*). The part becomes larger than the whole: a double enclave, an undecidable relation of inclusion that regulates the circulation of hits.

4. Capital's Intimate Hymn

1. "Il est interdit de passer / Par cette mélodie / Il est interdit de passer / Par cet air-là / Cette mélodie est privée / Strictement interdit danger . . . / Ce que cette mélodie me rappelle / C'est strictement confidentiel."
2. In a posthumous fragment titled "Capitalism as Religion," Benjamin wrote: "Freud's theory . . . is capitalist through and through. By virtue of a profound analogy, which has still to be illuminated, what has been repressed, the idea of sin, is capital itself, which pays interest on the hell of the unconscious." Benjamin, "Capitalism as Religion," trans. Rodney Livingstone, in *Walter Benjamin: Selected Writings*, 1:291.
3. See Véronique Mortaigne, "'What a Wonderful World' rayé des programmes radio et television," *Le Monde*, September 21, 2001. It should be noted in passing that this kind of censorship, coming not from the state but consensual enough to be efficient, is clearly not a prerogative of the United States. Proof of that can be found during the so-called "Gulf" war in France, as Véronique Mortaigne underlines in the same article: "In 1991, the Gulf war had quickly engendered a form of self-censorship of songs on the radio and television in France. . . . Lists of 'dangerous' songs and, in particular, of songs that spoke of war or peace, were drawn up for in-house use. A curious mix was proposed by these budding censors: Boris Vian's *The Deserter* was considered unwelcome in a war-path context, as was *When My Heart Goes Boom* by Charles Trenet. Véronique Sanson's *Allah* also suffered from this effort." (Translation mine.)
4. See John Baily, "Can You Stop the Birds Singing?" in *The Censorship of Music in Afghanistan* (Freemuse, http://www.freemuse.org, 2001). It is striking to read to what extent Taliban censorship focused on the amplification and the technological instruments of music. According to one of the testimonies cited by Baily (38), the Taliban burned "radio cassettes" in a public stadium; the reels from the cassettes were hung from trees (36).
5. This is in fact something that the juridical history of musical works seems to confirm. To limit ourselves to the case of France,

up until 1786, for "purely musical" works (that is to say works *without words*), it was not necessary to obtain a royal privilege or permission to engrave them. In other words, they were submitted to no form of explicit censorship. On the condition that the music did not transmit a *text* (no "message"), any author or editor of music could choose to engrave any piece of music he chose, until a September 1786 law put an end to this possibility.

6. Cited from the minutes of the 1866 "Select Parliamentary Committee on Theatrical Licenses and Regulations," by Roberta Montemorra Marvin, "The Censorship of Verdi's Operas in Victorian London," in *Music and Letters* 82, no. 4 (2001): 582.
7. On this point, see Georges Aperghis and Peter Szendy, *Wonderland: La musique, recto verso* (Paris: Bayard, 2004).
8. Luca Cerchiari, *Jazz e fascismo* (Palermo: L'Epos, 2003).
9. This is actually a cover, because the song, whose authors are Ahmet Ertegun and Betty Nelson, had already encountered a certain amount of success when it was sung by Ben E. King in 1962.
10. See http://www.amnestyusa.org/imagine/aboutimagine.html.
11. The music was written by Hoagy Carmichael, and the lyrics were written by Stuart Gorrell in 1930.
12. This is a nickname that itself comes from an old popular song, "Jump Jim Crow." It was first sung by the white actor Thomas Dartmouth "Daddy" Rice in 1828 and mocked Blacks by imitating their accent and caricaturing their customs, thus inaugurating the tradition of the minstrel show, with white artists made up as Blacks. To put it briefly, in Georgia, the "Jim Crow" laws imposed segregation, particularly in restaurants, until they were abolished in the 1960s.
13. Marcel Proust, *Swann's Way*, trans. C. K. Moncrieff and Terence Kilmartin (New York: Random House, 1980), 238.
14. See Philippe Grimbert, *Psychanalyse de la chanson* (Paris: Hachette, 2004), and Sigmund Freud, *Jokes and Their Relation to the Unconscious*, trans. and ed. James Strachey (New York: Norton, 1960).
15. Immanuel Kant, *Critique of Judgment*, trans. Nicolas Walker (New York: Oxford University Press, 1952), 148.
16. Ibid., 160.

17. Immanuel Kant, *The Metaphysics of Morals*, trans. and ed. Mary Gregor (Cambridge: Cambridge University Press, 1996), 69. I owe the comparison of *Witz* and money to Frederico Leoni and to our friendly discussion after his fine presentation, "The Community of Laughter and Living Money," in the proceedings of the colloquium *Communauté*, organized by the Parlement des Philosophes in Strasburg in May 2006.
18. I cannot avoid mentioning here the memory of the first time I heard "Money." I was nineteen at the time, and it happened on a beach in Crete. I couldn't walk on the hot sand all the way to the little tobacco store that was broadcasting hit music. Forced to take the path by the sea to buy cigarettes (also destined to go up in smoke and gas), I was carrying the little bit of money we had in a little folder attached to my forehead to keep it out of the water. Having become a strange conveyer of funds, I would give rhythm to my arm strokes with Pink Floyd's song.
19. Kant, *Metaphysics of Morals*, 76.
20. "Remember my name—Fame—I'm gonna live forever—I'm gonna learn how to fly—High . . . —I'm gonna make it to heaven—Light up the sky like a flame—Fame—I'm gonna live forever—Baby remember my name—Remember, remember, remember. . . ." [*Translator's note*: Having translated the lyrics to the French songs Szendy cites, I cannot help but underline how apt his description of this experience is.
21. "Cette année-là,/Je chantais pour la première fois./Le public ne me connaissait pas,/Quelle année cette année-là . . ./C'était hier, mais aujourd'hui rien n'a changé,/C'est le même métier qui ce soir recommence encore,/C'était l'année soixante-deux."
22. "Appunti per un videoclip mancato," in Vencenzo Mollica, *Fellini: Parole e disegni* (Turin: Einaudi, 2000), 20. The video was supposed to be for a song by Paul McCartney, formerly of the Beatles.

6. The Blood of the Cut and the Promise of the Breakthrough

1. This study first appeared thanks to Dragan Kujundcic in *Tympanum: A Journal of Comparative Literary Studies*, special issue:

"Khoraographies for Jacques Derrida," no. 4 (2000). The text was preceded by the following lines: "The following pages were written for a debate around Esteban Buch's book (*Beethoven's Ninth: A Political History* [Chicago: University of Chicago Press, 2004]) at the Ircam in Paris on May 20, 2000. Unexpectedly, Jacques Derrida honored us by discreetly slipping into the room to listen to our papers in silence. I dedicate this text to his friendship, with a postscriptum of several further questions."

2. Buch, *Beethoven's Ninth,* 221. Subsequent references will be by page number in parentheses in the text.
3. T. W. Adorno and Ernst Krenek, *Briefwechsel* (Frankfurt am Main: Suhrkamp, 1974). See also "De la musique en pédagogie de la musique. Lettre à Ernst Krenek," translated from the German by Jean Lauxerois and Peter Szendy, in *Enseigner la composition* (Paris: Ircam-L'Harmattan, 1999). (Translation mine.)
4. For details on this, as well as for a comparative analysis of Strauss's original and Schoenberg's arrangement, see Horst Weber, "'Melancholisch duerster Walzer, kommst mir nimmer aus den Sinnen!' Anmerkungen zu Schönbergs 'solistischer Instrumentation' des *Kaiserwalzers* von Johann Strauß," *Musik-Konzepte,* no. 36 (1984).
5. Edward Dannreuther, "Beethoven and His Works: A Study," *Macmillan's Magazine,* 34 (July 1876) (cited by K. M. Knittel, "Wagner, Deafness, and the Reception of Beethoven's Late Style," *Journal of the American Musicological Society* 51, no. 1 [1998]: 72). Dannreuther, who had translated Wagner's *Beethoven* into English, described Beethoven's late work as touching "upon the domain of the seer and the prophet," like a "saint" delivering "a message of religious love" (ibid., 71).
6. In this context, I cannot avoid recounting a recent experience of mine. I was invited to give a paper at the Philharmonic Orchestra of Strasburg on October 21, 1999, as an introduction to a concert whose program included Beethoven's Triple concerto opus 56 and Brahms's Fourth symphony as well as the "premiere" of Jorge Muniz Salas's APXH. The concert was funded in part by a group called "nouvelle musique en liberté" ("new music in liberty"). Jorge Muniz Salas, with his opus 52 ending (according to

the program's notes) in a "triumphant" C-major, was the winner of the "European competition for young composers" organized by the Circle of the Philharmonic Orchestra of Strasburg. In the preamble to the competition's rules, it was noted that "the signatories of the present letter, moved by a concern for their participation in the enrichment of contemporary European cultural heritage, are convinced that the Union of women and men of Europe will come about in particular thanks to the democratic access of every individual to culture, a harmonious means of friendship and comprehension among peoples." And in the third paragraph, "*Characteristics of the work submitted to the competition.* The work will have to last no more than 10 minutes. It will be exclusively symphonic. It will not bear any electro-acoustic additions. . . . Beyond the aforementioned obligations, composers will benefit from the most absolute aesthetic liberty [*sic*]. *Candidates must imperatively prepare for the possibility for the autonomous performance of a 2 minute fragment taken from their work, keeping in mind that this extract may become an official anthem.*" Emphasis mine, of course.

7. See *The Collected Writings of Rousseau*, ed. R. D. Masters and C. Kelly, 12 vols. (Hanover, N.H.: University Press of New England, 1990), 7:445.
8. Theodor W. Adorno, *Mahler: A Musical Physiognomy*, trans. Edmund Jephcott (Chicago: University of Chicago Press, 1996). Subsequent references to this work are by page number in parentheses in the text.
9. "The breakthrough (*Durchbruch*) in the First Symphony affects the entire form. The recapitulation to which it leads cannot restore the balance demanded by the sonata form. It shrinks to a hasty epilogue. The young composer's sense of form treats it as a coda, without thematic development of its own; the memory of the main idea drives the music swiftly to its end. But the abbreviation of the recapitulation is prepared by the exposition, which dispenses with multiplicity of forms and the traditional thematic dualism and so needs no complex restitution" (ibid., 5–6).
10. "Material," writes Adorno in his *Aesthetic Theory* (New York: Continuum, 2004), "is what artists work with: It is the sum of all

that is available to them, including words, colors, sounds, associations of every sort and every technique ever developed. To this extent, forms too can become material."

11. "Every artwork, even if it presents itself as a work of perfect harmony, is in itself the nexus of a problem. As such it participates in history and thus oversteps its own uniqueness" (ibid., 454).
12. I attempted a sketch of this deconstruction of the "work" in *Listen: A History of Our Ears*, trans. Charlotte Mandell (New York: Fordham University Press, 2008).

7. Da Capo: Follow the Notes

1. This fictive correspondence, destined to be a prelude for a reading of Kafka's "Josephine" (see next chapter), was published as a series of letters in *Resistances et utopies sonores: Musique et Politique au XXe siècle*, edited by Laurent Feneyrou (Paris: Cdmc, 2005).
2. "Voi siete qui, io sono qui. . . . Ognuno deve dedicare attenzione al suo istrumento. Solamente questo noi possiamo fare, adesso."
3. "Aggrappatevi alle note. Seguite le note. Una dopo altra. Cosi come mie mani vi possano indicare. Noi siamo musicisti. Voi siete musicisti. E siamo qui per riprovare. Niente paura. La prova va avanti. Vostri posti, signori. A vostri posti, prego."
4. "Noi dobbiamo i suoni dare un poco meno di colore. Forse è bene ricordare che rumore non è musica. . . . Dove siamo noi qua? Sopra di uno campo di calcio? Credete che io sono forse arbitro? E poi, ottoni, dove siete, cosa fate voi? Che succede ai vostri piccolo polmoni? Dove è andato vostro fiato? Tutto perduto in stupidi chiacchere?"
5. "Con forza soffiar! Mit Kraft! Diese Trompeten müssen die Toten aufwecken! . . . Seid ihr Musiker, oder nicht? Ich will einen Ton, der die Farbe des Feuers hat! Signori, *da capo!*"
6. *Prova d'orchestra* was shot in 1979 for Italian television. According to Fellini, the film was based on a chapter from Elias Canetti's *Crowds and Power* about the orchestra conductor. Some critics read it as "Fellini's reaction to the 1978 assassination of the Italian

politician Aldo Moro" (as Francesco Tornabene puts it in *Federico Fellini: Le réaliste du fantastique* [Cologne: Taschen, 1990]). Fellini nonetheless repeatedly denied any literal political or sociohistorical interpretation: "I didn't want to write a historical essay, or even a political or sociological essay. I didn't want to pronounce a condemnation of unions. It is the rehearsal of an orchestra, not of Italian history" (Fellini, "Le danger est en nous," in *Prova d'orchestra* [Geneva: Editions Albatros, 1979]). The composer Giorgio Battistelli based an opera with the same title on the film (see *Prova d'Orchestra, Giorgio Battistelli*, Opéra du Rhin program [Strasbourg, 1996]).

7. Cf. Peter Szendy, *Membres fantômes—des corps musiciens* (Paris: Minuit, 2002).
8. My translation: "Der Rattenfänger von Hameln /Durch die Stadt ist er gegangen /Hat mit seinem Pfeifen all die /Tausend Kindlein eingefangen."
9. "Der Rattenfänger von Hameln/Aus der Stadt wollt er sie retten/ Daß die Kindlein einen bessern/Ort zum Größerwerden hätten/ Er pfiff hübsch. Er pfiff lang./'s war ein wunderbarer Klang."
10. Vincenzo Mollica, *Fellini: Parole e disegni* (Turin: Einaudi, 2000).
11. [*Translator's note:* Szendy is punning on the expression for blackmail in French, which is "faire chanter" or literally, to make someone sing.]
12. "Apprunti per un videoclip mancato" (Mollica, *Fellini*, 20). These are notes for a video clip for a song by the ex-member of the Beatles, Paul McCartney.
13. Fellini himself declared that *Prova d'orchestra* is "an apology that was inspired by the 'Orchestra Conductor' in Elias Canetti's *Crowds and Power*, a monumental reflection on the nature of violence" (in *Federico Fellini. Sono un gran bugiardo*, texts gathered by Damian Pettigrew, Elleu Multimedia [Rome, 2003]). I have already proposed a reading of this text by Canetti in *Membres fantômes.*
14. "Die Straße, wodurch die Kinder zum Tor hinausgegangen, hieß noch in der Mitte des XVIII. Jahrhunderts (wohl noch heute) die bunge-lose (trommeltonlose, stille), weil kein Tanz darin geschehen noch Saitenspiel durfte gerührt werden." Robert Browning also incorporates this aspect.

15. Walter Benjamin, "Critique of Violence," trans. Edmund Jephcott, in *Walter Benjamin: Selected Writings*, 1:236–52.
16. Ibid., 248.

8. Kafka at the Star Academy*: Nothing's Anthem*

1. Published as a series in the journal *Vacarme*, no. 41 (2007) and no. 42 (2008). *Star Academy*, as anyone in France knows, is a reality show that started in April 2001 and followed the model of shows like NBC's *Fame* in the United States, *Pop Idol* in England (on ITV1), and *Saranno famosi* in Italy. Young singers selected for the show were filmed over the course of their training before presenting numbers for weekly competitions, over the course of which the audience was asked to vote to elect the best candidate.
2. Franz Kafka, "Josefine, die Sängerin oder das Volk der Mäuse." The English translation, sometimes modified, is by Willa Muir and Edwin Muir (New York: Schocken, 1971), 360–76. Subsequent references to this work are given by page number in parentheses in the text.
3. "An ordinary farmhand can keep it up effortlessly all day long, besides doing his work," the narrator says somewhere about the piping of mice in general.

9. Musicology and Melology: Prince, Eros, and Copyright

1. This article first appeared as a series in the journal *Vacarme*, nos. 43, 44 (2008).
2. I am borrowing this word from Berlioz, who used it to describe his piece *Lélio*, which was both sung and spoken, between melodrama and cantata.
3. "Pendant le temps, dans le temps de ma chanson, / Elle coule, coule, l'eau, sous les ponts du monde, / Des hommes naissent et puis d'autres s'en vont / Dans le temps de ma chanson, dans le temps de ma chanson."
4. On the 1986 album *Ornella e . . .* : "Un applauso del pubblico pagante lo sottolineerà / E dalla bocca del cannone una canzone

suonerà/E con le mani amore per le mani ti prenderò/E senza dire parole nel mio cuore ti porterò."

5. Anthumous and not posthumous in effect, since it is before his death that the song's "I" sees itself both buried and resurrected in the phonographic grooves: "Dance to me/The night of my funeral./Let life be a fireworks/And death a brushfire./A swan song has died out/But another has broken the egg./Under a sapphire in real sapphire/A new groove sparkles." ("Dansez sur moi /Le soir de mes funerailles./Que la vie soit un feu d'artifice/Et la mort un feu de paille./Un chant de cygne s'est éteint/Mais un autre a cassé l'œuf./Sous un saphir en vrai saphir/Miroite mon sillon neuf.")
6. "Something that keeps sticking to my heart and my body" ("*Un truc qui m'colle encore au cœur et au corps*"): This is the sentence that, at the end of each verse, introduces a citation of, for example, the Beatles' 1964 *A Hard Day's Night.*
7. Michael Heatley, *Where Were You . . . When the Music Played? 120 Unforgettable Moments in Music History* (New York: Penguin, 2008).
8. The rapper Chuck D., for example, to whom Prince pays homage by naming him in "Musicology," goes further than the simple reappropriation of his *own* rights, since he is one of the most vigorous defenders of peer-to-peer distribution. (See www.wired .com, "Rappers in Disharmony on P2P.")
9. Walter Benjamin, "The Paris of the Second Empire in Baudelaire," in *Selected Writings,* 4:33.

10. This Is It: The King of Pop

1. This piece first appeared in Italian in *Pop filosofia*, ed. Simone Regazzoni (Genoa: Il Melangolo, 2010). I thank Simone Regazzoni for his generous invitation to think about what "pop philosophy" might mean.
2. Of course we all know that in 1994 this King of Pop married Lisa Marie Presley, the daughter of the King of Rock 'n' Roll, before getting divorced in 1996. An analysis of the representation of sovereignty in so-called popular music needs to be undertaken.

During the funeral of James Brown, himself nicknamed "The Godfather of Soul," Michael Jackson embraced the deceased body of someone who was a true model for him (see Chas Newkey-Burden, *Michael Jackson: Legend 1958–2009* [London: Michael O'Mara Books, 2009], 182). We should also remember the 1983 concert when James Brown first called Michael Jackson up on stage, followed by . . . Prince. In addition, as Pascal Bertin notes in the special 2009 edition of *Les Inrockuptibles* devoted to Michael Jackson, on the 1995 *2 Bad*, the King of Pop used a sample of "a few words and the bass-line rhythm of 'King of Rock' from the second album by the group Run-DMC that had appeared ten years earlier. In the video released at the time, the hip-hop duo threw down Michael Jackson's sequined glove to trample it and win their title of King of Rock" (25).

3. See Newkey-Burden, *Michael Jackson,* 189. The previously cited special edition of *Les Inrockuptibles* devoted to Michael Jackson even opened with a series of articles called "More Popular than Jesus Christ." We know that in 1985, Michael Jackson bought the rights to the catalogue of most of the songs by the Beatles. "More Popular than Jesus Christ" was a quip pronounced by John Lennon that caused quite a stir when, in March 1966 at the height of Beatlemania, he declared to a British journalist from the *Evening Standard*: "Christianity will go. It will vanish and shrink. I needn't argue about that: I'm right, and I will be proved right. We're more popular than Jesus Christ now: I don't know which will go first—rock 'n' roll or Christianity." (See also "Rock 'n' Roll: According to John," *Time*, August 12, 1966 www.time.com). On November 22, 2008, the Vatican's newspaper *L'Osservatore romano* "pardoned" the ex-Beatle who was assassinated in 1980.
4. See the report in the August 9, 2009, edition of *Libération*: "The museum's curator Jim Phillips said staff had been 'inundated' with inquiries from Jackson fans since the star's similarities to the bust were pointed out in a recent newspaper article. 'We've had people coming to the museum and asking "Where's Michael Jackson?" So we have to tell them that he's not here, but there is a bust that looks a lot like him,' Phillips told AFP."
5. Cf. "Jackson's Face 'Appears on Toast,'" on the BBC News website (http://www.bbc.co.uk/news/), June 21, 2005.

6. Michael Jackson, *Moonwalk* (New York: Harmony Books, 1988), 264.
7. In his beautiful afterword to my *Prophecies of Leviathan: Reading Past Melville* (New York: Fordham University Press, 2009), Gil Anidjar speaks of a "narcissism of the other thing." The following pages owe much to what Gil Anidjar allowed me to read from his current work, much of it yet to be published, toward a "critique of Christianity." One can gain a partial perception of this project in "Blutgewalt," *Oxford Literary Review* 31 (December 2009): 153–74, and "The Idea of an Anthropology of Christianity" in *interventions* 11, no. 3 (2009): 367–93.
8. See Marc Shell, *Art and Money* (Chicago: University of Chicago Press, 1995), 15: "The Eucharist wafer is conceptually numismatic," he notes after having recalled that "the wafer was expressly manufactured like a coin: it was pressed between wafer irons and impressed with insignia like those of coins."
9. Mark C. Taylor affirms this in *Confidence Games: Money and Markets in a World without Redemption* (Chicago: University of Chicago Press, 2004), 68. Taylor references Shell, even if Shell simply says that "the sign of the new dollar had a form noticeably like that of the . . . HIS" (Shell, *Art and Money*, 147n59).
10. See Giorgio Agamben, *Le Règne et la gloire*, French trans. Joël Gayraud and Marin Rueff (Paris: Seuil, 2008), passim.
11. Walter Benjamin, "Capitalism as Religion," trans. Rodney Livingstone, in *Walter Benjamin: Selected Writings*, 1:290. Whoever seeks to engage with this enigmatic text by Benjamin would not be able to forgo reading Samuel Weber's remarkable analyses of it in "Closing the Net," in *Benjamin's–abilities* (Cambridge, Mass.: Harvard University Press, 2008), 250–80.
12. Max Weber, *The Protestant Ethic and the Spirit of Capitalism*, trans. Talcott Parsons (1958; Mineola, N.Y.: Dover, 2003), 48.
13. Benjamin, "Capitalism as Religion," 1:288.
14. By taking the King of Pop as an object of philosophical discourse and citing Walter Benjamin and a few others in order to think through his passion for and in exchange, does this mean we are doing "*pop philosophy*"? Gilles Deleuze and Félix Guattari are the first to have spoken of "pop philosophy," for example in *Kafka:*

For a Minor Literature, trans. Dana Polan (Minneapolis: University of Minnesota Press, 1986), 26–27. "What we call pop—pop music, pop philosophy, pop writing. . . . To make use of the polylingualism of one's own language, to make a minor or intensive use of it, to oppose the oppressed quality of this language to its oppressive quality." If a pop-philosophical discourse on the King of Pop must let itself be contaminated by its object—one that is therefore not a simple object—there is no indication that this contamination can be grasped in the terms of the opposition oppressed versus oppressor (when one speaks of a pop passion such as Michael's, these positions *are constantly exchanging* one another in a vertiginous way; they go mad in their exchange). The expression and project implicit in Deleuze's "pop-philosophy" has been taken up since then by others: in France, for example, by Elie During and Patrice Maniglier in the collective work *Matrix: Philosophical Machine* (Paris: Ellipses, 2003, with the notable collaboration of Alain Badiou). In the collection *Fresh Theory* (Paris: Léo Scheer, 2005), During and Maniglier return to the premises of their endeavor in an interview titled "What's Left Of Pop'philosophy?" There, they say that "the problem behind pop'philosophy" is that of "the impure hooks or shifters that philosophy gives itself as a way to start." In other words, the practice of philosophy finds its starting point and anchor in something nonphilosophical: "Alongside an entire line of thinkers (Nietzsche, Marx, Freud, Deleuze . . .), we believe that, from the point of view of philosophy, philosophical engagement is always impure. In other words, in spite of everything one might tell oneself on the subject, it is always bad reasons that bring us to philosophy. There is a necessary heterogeneity to the conditions of philosophy: it is always for bad reasons that one does it, for reasons that are hardly 'philosophical.'" For several years now, the expression has spread and the media can now call a philosopher such as Slavoj Žižek a "star of pop philosophy" (see in particular *Philosophie Magazine*, no. 8 [2007]). Publishers such as Open Court Publishing in the United States have launched collections called "Popular Culture and Philosophy" (whose first title appeared in 2000), with innumerable titles in the style of

Star Wars and Philosophy, James Bond and Philosophy, Monty Python and Philosophy . . . Whatever you want *and Philosophy*? Philosophy applied to all objects available on the market? Philosophy that is applied more than it is invented? If one fully understands During and Maniglier, it is the exact opposite: "Pop philosophy" is not a fully constituted thought applied to different objects of "popular culture": Quite to the contrary, it is thinking that seeks itself, philosophically, *on the basis of* its exposition to the impure. And by letting itself be profoundly, *passionately*, affected by it. Or *infected* by it, as Laura Odello has put it ("*Il Regno è infetto*," in *Pop filosofia*), to find itself transformed, to *mutate* as Simone Regazzoni suggests (ibid.). By letting itself be invaded by the impure, then, including its own language, but in an intralinguistic polylingualism where oppression, we would emphasize, is difficult to *situate*. This leaves the very term "popular," whose weighted metaphysical presuppositions have been analyzed by Jacques Derrida, most notably in his reading of Kant (see "Popularities: On the Right to the Philosophy of Right," trans. Peggy Kamuf, in *Eyes of the University* [Stanford: Stanford University Press, 2004], 175–82). Might it be that, with or starting with Benjamin, one might imagine something like "pop" objects that are neither simply objects nor determined by their being relegated, even implicitly, to the entirely problematic conception of a "people"? In order to find an answer to this inquiry, one would have to start with certain benjaminian passages I cited at the beginning of this book, and in particular the posthumous 1929 fragment called "Some Remarks on Folk Art," which concludes with this note: "Folk art and kitsch allow us to look outward *from within objects*" (279). It would no doubt be necessary to begin to reinterrogate the Thing, by rereading Heidegger. And such a rereading would probably have to critically encounter the work of Graham Harman and several others who lay claim to an "object-oriented philosophy." These are open questions, already exceeding the context of an overextended endnote.

15. As Sam Weber writes in *Benjamin's–abilities* (254), "Capitalism takes the cult to the extreme . . . by allowing it to become its own source of meaning, that is, by endowing it with a certain autonomy."

16. Benjamin, "Capitalism as Religion," 1:288–89. [Translation modified: *Schuld* can be translated as both "debt" and "guilt," and the economic register is much more resonant with Szendy's argument here.]

17. One of his biographers (Chas Newkey-Burden, *Michael Jackson*, 183) writes: "One of the biggest surprises of Michael's latter years was the way one of the most successful entertainers of all time, who had sold 750 million records, found himself in such colossal debt. How could this happen? The story began to unravel during his 2005 trial, in which prosecutors had described him as a 'spendaholic' who had a 'billionaire spending habit for only a millionaire's spending budget.' His spending had exceeded his income for decades, and an accountant gave evidence that the annual deficit was up to $30 million."